Praise for His Power, Our Weakness

"An honest and encouraging book written specifically for biblical counselors. Beth hits on the struggles and discouragements encountered by everyone who counsels and provides biblical encouragement and exhortation to continue serving God's people in personal soul care."

- Don Roy, DMin, ACBC Fellow, IBCD Training Center Director, Slidell, LA

"Whether you're a seasoned biblical counselor with years of experience or new to biblical counseling, you have or will experience doubts, regrets, or discouragement. Through her own personal experiences, Beth Ann Baus points to the One who helps our unbelief, redeems our past mistakes, and gives hope for transformed lives through biblical counseling."

- Lisa Berg, serving Community Bible Church in High Point, NC

"Counseling the counselor. Encouraging the encourager. Equipping the equipper. Beth Ann Baus has written an uplifting and practical template for biblical counselors that includes topics we seldom discuss. I believe every Christian counselor will find this book insightful, helpful, practical, encouraging, and inspiring. "

- Ellen Olivetti, Director of Counseling, Pathways Counseling Center, Fishers, IN

"This book tackles issues biblical counselors might face personally while encouraging the counselor with God's Word. It greatly encouraged me!

Beth points biblical counselors to God and not themselves. By using her own experiences as examples, she lovingly guides the biblical counselor to Christ for hope and helps with issues a biblical counselor might face."

- Vara Castleberry, serving Christ Presbyterian Church, Brentwood, TN

"This book uniquely promotes spiritual growth of the biblical counselor by offering examples of relatable challenges, giving prompts for personal reflection, providing ample encouragement, and directing the reader to apply practical, biblical tools."

- Jodi Ekk, serving Christ City Church, Vancouver, Canada

"[After reading *His Power, Our Weakness*] My heart has been encouraged as I remembered God's character and His wondrous grace towards me and the counselees. He has called me to place His character at the forefront of every wilderness-like trial and season of suffering. My soul has a new resolve to persevere, depending upon the grace and faithfulness of God to carry me when my own life and that of the counselees cause heaviness of heart. God is the hope, strength, and eternal treasure of our lives (counselor and counselee together)."

- Shalika Young, serving through Restore Hope in Hampton, VA.

His Power, Our Weakness

Encouragement for the Biblical Counselor

by

Beth Ann Baus

To my husband, Chad.
The one who consistently encourages me
by pointing to the source of all encouragement.

acknowledgements

Thank you to Renee Pitman, Marilyn Smith, and Ashley Zimmerman for sharing your experiences. It's a joy to see the Lord work in and through each of you.

Thank you, Sam Holdsambeck, for dotting the i's and crossing the t's. Your insight added depth to this work and, for that, I am exceedingly grateful.

Thank you, Andrea Boeyink, for sharing your artistic talents. Your art inspires me.

contents

a note from the author

I enter each and every counseling session very aware of my inadequacies and in full reliance on the Holy Spirit to lead the session. I look at my counselees with great humility, knowing that my need for the Lord Jesus Christ is just as deep as theirs and that my wandering heart desires to satisfy the flesh just as theirs do.

It is with that same awareness that I present this work to you. I am well aware that I have much growing to do as a person and certainly as a biblical counselor. I pray this work will serve as a tool for you, and myself, as we humbly serve in this labor of love.

While this was written specifically for the biblical counselor with the intent of encouraging you in your work, I believe this book would also benefit the mentor, discipleship leader, small group leader, or anyone serving in any capacity that involves pouring into another person with the intent of soul care.

This book displays personal accounts and therefore names and some details have been changed to protect the privacy of the counselees. I pray these stories will resonate with you and help you in your own ministry. I genuinely believe that one way the Lord redeems our struggles is by allowing them to be shared, in the context of learning from them and marveling at how the Lord works through them.

Just as we biblical counselors do not labor in vain, our counselees do not struggle in vain.

May the Lord grant you growth in your knowledge and understanding of him. May he allow his Holy Spirit to guide your counseling sessions and bring about change in the lives of your counselees. May he, in his perfect timing, bring this book before you to offer you encouragement and to remind you that his power is made perfect in our weakness.

Our ministries exist not simply for the purpose of helping people live well now; our ministries, like our whole lives, must aim for the end, when we'll see Jesus face-to-face.

Gloria Furman, Word Filled Women's Ministry

Chapter 1

Regretting the Past

In the gospel the knowledge of our acceptance in Christ makes it easier to admit that we are flawed, because we know we won't be cast off if we confess the true depths of our sinfulness.

Tim Keller

What excited me the most as I went through the certification process to become a Biblical Counselor was finally learning how to utilize my Bible. With every training session I sat through, it was like light bulb after light bulb was coming on. The Spirit was illuminating scripture for me in a new way, and for the first time in my life, I understood how to use the Word and apply it to everyday problems. For instance, I can't tell you how many times I've read the book of Ephesians. But I could never have explained to anyone the idea of "put off - put on." I can't tell you how many times I've read the account of Joseph, yet it never occurred to me to point someone who had experienced abuse or mistreatment to this story and help them see the amazing, godly response that Joseph had toward his brothers. I actually remember feeling quite stupid. I couldn't believe this book of tools had been in my hands my entire life and yet I had no idea how to use it!

Once I moved past feeling stupid and just enjoyed learning and began practicing putting the Word to use, I was overcome with sadness. I thought back to all the years I spent pouring into different women and trying to counsel them, and realized I had been doing it wrong. I realized I had been giving those women my opinion, with a little bit of "God talk" mixed in. I was ashamed, embarrassed, and actually spent time in prayer asking God to allow those women to forget all the terribly wrong things I had said to them.

Let me give you an example. A sweet young woman came to me because she was convicted of her sexual sin. She and her fiance, both of whom claimed to be Christians, were actively engaging in sexual activity and she wanted me to help her break this habit. Here are some of the areas where I royally messed up:

- I didn't gather data or ask questions. I started with her current sexual sin and went straight into talking about consequences.

- Instead of taking her to the Bible I gave her my opinion. Now, in my defense, my opinion was based on biblical truth, but nonetheless, I took her to the book of Beth rather than the Word of God.

- Instead of speaking truth in love, I spoke harshly. In fact, I was so harsh I made her cry.

- I had zero compassion. When she cried I sat before her with pride over convicting her of her sin.

- I gave no acknowledgement to the Spirit and the work *HE* was doing.

- I didn't take her to Jesus and remind her of his radical gift of forgiveness.

- Instead of offering her hope, I handed her a plate of judgment.

This list could go on and on, but you get the idea. The amazing thing is, she kept coming back! Even after I told her that she had given up her right to wear a white wedding dress. (I'm literally hanging my head in shame as I write these words.) There was absolutely no love, no compassion, no pointing to Jesus who gave his life to forgive her of her sins. There was, however, plenty of judgment, condemnation, harshness and hostility.

While I was going through a season of regretting my past in the counseling room, I shared this story with a dear friend of mine, and here's what she said:

> Don't tell yourself that you were doing it *wrong* all those years. Tell yourself you just weren't as effective as you will be moving forward. You were trying to be faithful back then. You were trying to help those women. So stop beating yourself up. Now you've got the tools to properly utilize the Word. Move forward with confidence that the Lord will redeem your mistakes and celebrate the fact that he's giving you a second chance at this with a fuller understanding of what he wants you to do.

My dear friend was living out 1 Thessalonians 5:11, which tells us to encourage one another and build one another up. What a blessing it was to hear these words. If she had followed my example from years ago, she would have pointed her finger in my face and told me I should be ashamed of myself, that I shouldn't consider myself worthy of counseling, and that I had, in fact, given up my right to speak into the lives of other women. Praise God she had more wisdom than I. Praise God what she had to say was encouraging and uplifting.

If you're like me and you're deeply embarrassed by your past, if you've said things in the counseling room that you regret, if you desperately wish you could turn back time, take your words back and start over, please listen to my friend. Stop beating yourself up. Move forward with the tools you've been given and move forward in confidence that God will show you how to use them.

When I think back on my early years of informal counseling, I think of Moses. Consider Numbers 20:2-13.

> *Now there was no water for the congregation. And they assembled themselves together against Moses and against Aaron. And the people quarreled with Moses and said, "Would that we had perished when our brothers perished before the Lord! Why have you brought the assembly of the Lord into this wilderness, that we should die here, both we and our cattle? And why have you made us come up out of Egypt to bring us to this evil place? It is no place for grain or figs or vines or pomegranates, and there is no water to drink." Then Moses and Aaron went from the presence of the assembly to the entrance of the tent of meeting and fell on their faces. And the glory of the Lord appeared to them, and the Lord spoke to Moses, saying, "Take the staff, and assemble the congregation, you and Aaron your brother, and tell the rock before their eyes to yield its water. So you shall bring water out of the rock for them and give drink to the congregation and their cattle." And Moses took the staff from before the Lord, as he commanded him.*
>
> *Then Moses and Aaron gathered the assembly together before the rock, and he said to them, "Hear now, you rebels: shall we bring*

water for you out of this rock?" And Moses lifted up his hand
and struck the rock with his staff twice, and water came out
abundantly, and the congregation drank, and their livestock. And
the Lord said to Moses and Aaron, "Because you did not believe
in me, to uphold me as holy in the eyes of the people of Israel,
therefore you shall not bring this assembly into the land that I
have given them." These are the waters of Meribah, where the
people of Israel quarreled with the Lord, and through them he
showed himself holy.

Do you see that? God told Moses to speak to the rock and tell the rock
to yield its water. But what did Moses do? He went rogue. Instead of
speaking to the rock as God instructed him, he struck the rock twice
with his staff. Like Moses, I thought I knew best. Even though it's true
that I knew the Word, I was yet to be trained in how to utilize it. I grew
up in church - in fact, my dad was a minister. So I can't claim ignorance
to what the scriptures say. All I can claim is my own sin.
Just as Moses failed to believe in God and the instructions he was given,
I failed to believe in the effectiveness of God's Word. I thought my
opinion on every matter was more relevant and more convincing than
opening my Bible and letting God speak for himself.

Have you read Stephen Viars' *Putting Your Past in Its Place?* If not, I
highly recommend it. I have gone through this book with multiple
counselees and have found it profoundly helpful each and every time.
But I found that Viars' book wasn't just for the counselee, it was for me
too. This passage from chapter three is right on target:

> The Bible gives us several ways our pasts can be among
> our best friends. Of course your past is not an "it." It is
> not a separate entity. But it is a record, in part, of the
> way God has related to you and worked in your life.

The goal is not to focus on "it" but on who God is and what He has done.[1]

Viars' thoughts on this were especially helpful to me as I fervently tried to take my thoughts captive, as instructed by 2 Corinthians 10:5. Now, when I find myself replaying the ridiculous things I have said to those women in the past, I remind myself to stop, and instead of focusing on "it," I remind myself to focus on who God is and what He has done.

God is our faithful, merciful Father who loves us too much to leave us in our sin. He changes us. He grows us up. That should be our focus when we find ourselves stuck in the past. And when we find ourselves hanging our head in shame for the careless words we've spoken and dread the day we are asked to give an account, we can have hope. We can point to Jesus, now and then, and know our sins have been forgiven.

What encourages me about this passage in Numbers 20 is that even though Moses disobeyed God, God was still faithful and gave water to his people. In the same way, I know I was not being obedient to God in how I counseled women all those years ago, yet in God's immeasurable grace, I have had women tell me how much they were helped by our time together all those years ago. And when I hear that, all I can do is point to God because it was he and he only doing the work. Only our great God could take the ridiculous words that came from my mouth and turn them into something worth hearing. Despite my disobedience, God still gave those women water.

While Moses was punished for his disobedience, God still used him in mighty ways. Imagine being blatantly disobedient yet still being given

---

[1] Stephen Viars, *Putting Your Past in Its Place: Moving Forward in Freedom and Forgiveness* (Eugene, Oregon: Harvest House Publishers, 2011), 48.

the privilege of introducing the Ten Commandments! This brings me *so* much comfort and *so* much encouragement. To know that I can fall short and be disobedient and the Lord still sees fit to use me . . . well, that just makes me want *all the more* to fall at his feet and worship!

What's in your toolbox?

Now that my toolbox actually holds tools and not just my own arrogance, I know how to combat the mistakes of my past. I have also learned that it's not enough to have a toolbox, nor is it enough to have a toolbox full of tools. We must put those tools to good use. I encourage you to dig around in your toolbox on a regular basis for *your* benefit, not just for the benefit of your counselee.

1.   Proverbs 18:13

"If one gives an answer before he hears, it is his folly and shame."

Data gathering is about more than taking notes, it's about listening. It's about listening so intently that you know what follow-up questions to ask, what points to come back to and what dots to connect to better understand the person in front of you. When we start counseling before we hear what the counselee has to share, we're exposing our own folly and shame.

2.   Hebrews 4:12

"For the word of God is living and active, sharper than any two-edged sword, piercing to the division of soul and of spirit, of joints and of marrow, and discerning the thoughts and intentions of the heart."

Ummm . . . why on earth did I think my opinion would be more effective than God's Word?

3. Ephesians 4:15

"Rather, speaking the truth in love, we are to grow up in every way into him who is the head, into Christ."

I knew this. I was very familiar with Ephesians 4:15, yet I thought my being blunt and harsh would be more effective than being soft-spoken and kind. (Again, I'm hanging my head in shame as I write this.) What God has taught me is that Jesus, while blunt and forthright, was never harsh. When he confronted the woman at the well, he didn't tell her she had given up her right to a white wedding dress. He offered her living water.

4. Lamentations 3:22-23

"The steadfast love of the Lord never ceases; his mercies never come to an end; they are new every morning; great is your faithfulness."

During this time when I was counseling with a hard heart and a lack of compassion, a dear friend felt led to confront me about the anger she could see in my heart. She pointed out how my anger was spilling out in other areas of my life without my realizing it, leading me to live my life with no compassion towards others. She pointed me to Lamentations 3:22-23 and reminded me that the NIV says, "His compassions never fail." She lovingly told me that since I claimed Christ as my savior then I should be striving to look less like me and more like him. She told me that if *his* mercies - if *his* compassions are new every morning, then *mine* had to be too. What would we do without dear friends who show us our blind spots?

5. John 16:7-8

"Nevertheless, I tell you the truth: it is to your advantage that I go away, for if I do not go away, the Helper will not come to you. But if I go, I will send him to you. And when he comes, he will convict the world concerning sin and righteousness and judgment."

I have to remind myself often that while I am very capable of making someone feel bad about a personal sin, I am not and never will be able to convict someone of sin. Might the Lord work through me to help someone see a blind spot and therefore be convicted? Absolutely, but even then, it's not me doing the work. The work of convicting any of us of our sins is always done by the Holy Spirit. This truth frees me from a responsibility I had put on myself and rids me of the pride that so easily sneaks in when change comes about in the counseling room.

6. 1 John 3:16

"By this we know love, that he laid down his life for us, and we ought to lay down our lives for the brothers."

An older woman in my church family often says, "How can any of us ever feel ignored? Whether we're married or single, we'll never hear words as romantic as the words of Jesus. He woos us every minute of every day." It took me a while to see Jesus' words as romantic, but I see it now. She isn't talking about the chocolate and roses kind of romance; she's talking about the deep, undying, steadfast love that only Jesus has for us. It is a love so deep, so genuine, so radical, that he not only forgave us our most grievous sins, but he took those heinous acts on himself and took the punishment in our place.

Have you ever wanted someone to love you so much that they would literally give their life for you? Well, Jesus did. His story - our story - is the story that inspires all other romantic stories. Why would I not, immediately, point my counselee to this great love?

7. Matthew 12:36

"I tell you, on the day of judgment people will give account for every careless word they speak."

If I were going to get a tattoo on the back of my hand to serve as a daily reminder of something, it might be this. I shudder to think that while I sat across from this young woman, who was made in the image of God, doling out judgment on her for her sin, I gave zero consideration to the fact that I must one day give an account for the careless words that were coming out of my mouth. Lord have mercy on me.

I can still picture that young woman sitting before me, fearful that her sin was unforgivable and that she was too far gone to change. If I could turn back time and have those conversations over again, I would point her to Isaiah 43:1-3, "Do not fear, for I have redeemed you; I have summoned you by name; you are mine. When you pass through the waters, I will be with you; and when you pass through the rivers, they will not sweep over you. When you walk through the fire, you will not be burned; the flames will not set you ablaze. For I am the LORD your God, the Holy One of Israel, your Savior…" Again, more romantic words have never been spoken.

Encouragement

If you haven't figured it out already, every bit of God's Word that you share with a counselee applies to you too. So, ask yourself - what are some ways you would apply God's Word to encourage counselees who regret their past?

- **He is faithful to forgive.**

Meditate on 1 John 1:9, "If we confess our sins, he is faithful and just to forgive us our sins and to cleanse us from all unrighteousness."

Someone once told me that regret is different from shame or guilt. Regret is like a history book. It serves as a reminder to not do that thing again which you once did and now regret doing. If you regret how you have counseled in the past, consider that regret a gift of God's grace. Think of it as a way of reminding you not to repeat that behavior going forward.

Perhaps you have more than regret. Maybe you know in your heart, in your thinking, through your actions, through your misuse of the Word that you were sinning in many ways. There is no greater encouragement than to know the Spirit has convicted you of your sin, that you can confess that sin, and that your Heavenly Father is faithful and just to forgive.

- **Yes, you can change.**

Meditate on Ephesians 4:22-24, "[you were taught in him] to put off your old self, which belongs to your former manner of life and is corrupt through deceitful desires, and to be renewed in the spirit of your minds, and to put on the new self, created after the likeness of God in true righteousness and holiness."

Something I realize now when I look back on those early years of counseling is that I was angry at those women and at their sin. But I confess, it wasn't a righteous anger; it was an anger born out of the fact that I could see pieces of myself and my own sin in all of them. Every time I sat across from a woman who had come to me for help, it was like looking in a mirror. And it made me angry.

If, like me, you have reacted poorly to a counselee, ask yourself why. Why did you lose your patience? Why were you angry? Why were you critical? Why were you lacking compassion? Ask God to search your heart and to show you why you responded the way you did.

Praise God that change is possible. We don't have to be what we once were! Rather than sitting in our sin and being angry at the corruptive nature of it, we can change. We can walk away, we can turn, we can begin again with a new self being created after the likeness of God.

- **God can redeem our past mistakes.**

Meditate on Isaiah 55:10-11, "For as the rain and the snow come down from heaven and do not return there but water the earth, making it bring forth and sprout, giving seed to the sower and bread to the eater, so shall my word be that goes out from my mouth; it shall not return to me empty, but it shall accomplish that which I purpose, and shall succeed in the thing for which I sent it."

I pray you find great encouragement in knowing that God can work through your sin. God can take your words that were so full of arrogance and toss them to the side, only allowing the nuggets of truth from his Word to penetrate the heart of the hearer.

However, that's only one side of the coin. The other way God redeems our past is by allowing the Spirit to convict us of our sin. Left on our own, we would continue to "help" people the way we have in the past. But God, who abounds in grace more than we can even comprehend, allows us to see our sinful ways. He shows us that we were, in some cases, doing more harm than good, but he then shows us that even then, we were working under his sovereign will and he will use what he wants of that time for his good purposes. Praise be to God!

Personal Reflection

1. What are some new ways you've learned to utilize your Bible since becoming a Biblical Counselor?

2. Write about a time when you counseled based on your opinion rather than God's Word.

3. Looking back, how would you handle that differently?

4. What scripture do you think would best encourage a counselee to let go of past regrets?

5. What scriptures do you turn to when your own past regrets weigh you down?

6. How do you think God might redeem the mistakes you've made in the counseling room?

Chapter 2

I'm changing. Why aren't you?

I'm not yet finished changing and growing, for I hope to never be satisfied with who I am in Christ until either he takes me home or he returns.

Brad Bigney, *Gospel Treason*

My dad was a gospel preacher for almost forty years, and I was always a bit intimidated by his biblical knowledge. As a child, I thought my dad was just born with this knowledge lodged in his brain and so it was logical that he chose the path of ministry. I mean, what else would you do with all that knowledge? As I got older, I began to understand this better. Just as we aren't sinners because we sin, but rather we sin because we're sinners, my dad wasn't a preacher because he had all this knowledge, he had all this knowledge because he was a preacher.

Have you ever given a speech, taught a class or written a paper or essay on a particular subject? You momentarily become a bit of an expert on that topic because in order to present the material thoroughly, you have to do your homework, you have to research and study. In order to be an effective teacher, you first must be a student. And this is exactly what happens when you train as a biblical counselor. You must learn the information for yourself before you can pass it on to your counselees.

Confession: I've always had a bit of an anger problem. Well, if I'm being honest it's more of a ginormous rage problem. Early in my marriage my husband got to see the full fury of my rage. Then when our children came along, I had one of those mirroring moments when my oldest son wanted to play house, where he was the mom and I was the child. What do you think he did? He yelled at me. He wasn't being disrespectful, he was pretending to be the mom and in his little world, the mom yelled. That was over fifteen years ago and it still makes me emotional to think about. Praise God for not leaving us in our sin! He changes us!

Over the years I learned to control my anger by keeping it pent up inside. In fact, as my boys got older and we started enjoying the Marvel movies as a family, I compared myself to the Incredible Hulk. There's a scene in The Avengers where the city is under attack and Captain America says to Dr. Banner, "Now might be a really good time for you to get angry." (In case you aren't familiar with this franchise, Captain America needed Dr. Banner, a seemingly normal man, to get angry and turn into the gigantic green monster known as the Incredible Hulk in order to fight the enemy and help save the city.) This is when Banner says one of his most famous lines, "That's my secret, Cap. I'm always angry."

This is how I lived my life. In order to keep my ugly green monster at bay, I had to live in a constant state of anger. When I made this comparison to my sons, they both commented on how they didn't understand, because to them, I was never angry. I told them two things: First, I was unbelievably grateful they didn't remember all my years of putting my anger on display. Second, if they could only see inside my heart, they'd see a different story. Let me just say here that I thought this was as good as it got. I thought this was the big change. God had changed me into a closet rager and I was happy with that. This is a perfect example of my limited faith. I was simply settling for less than God's best. Looking back I realize I was that ignorant child C.S. Lewis talked about who "wants to go on making mud pies in a slum because he cannot imagine what is meant by the offer of a holiday at sea."[2] I was far too easily pleased.

Praise God he didn't leave me in the slum with my mud pies. He kept working in me. I entered into the world of biblical counseling as a closet rager and I came out the other side with a heart so soft and tender I could hardly recognize myself. In fact, I had bouts of anxiety over not feeling like me! I wasn't used to the feeling of freedom and not being constantly weighed down by the crippling effects of my sin. Suddenly my mind was clear, my thoughts weren't racing with frustrations and my blood wasn't boiling. It was miraculous. In fact, my husband loves to laugh at me now when I attempt to yell. Even raising my voice to get someone's attention from across the house is a failed attempt. God, in an answer to my prayer, literally took away my ability to yell. Now, my feeble attempts to yell simply result in my voice raising an octave. It's silly, and it makes us laugh. But, deep down, I know that our laughter is also a form of praise. God did a miraculous thing in me.

While this is the most noticeable change that took place in me, it's far from the only one. Inwardly I found that I was suddenly less offended by my husband's authoritative voice. I was less annoyed when our sons didn't do exactly what I asked them to do exactly when I asked them to do it. I found myself feeling a longing to be with the very people that I used to avoid, my heart softening towards strained relationships, and I found myself having empathy for someone in my life who had abused me for many years. Outwardly I was becoming more emotional. I found myself laughing more, crying more, and having overall awareness of not only what I was feeling, but why I was feeling it. God was using this training to sanctify me in ways I didn't even know needed sanctifying. Suddenly I was aware of how judgmental I was, how I kept records of

---

[2] C. S. Lewis, *The Weight of Glory and Other Addresses* (Grand Rapids: William B. Eerdmans Publishing Company, 1965), 2.

wrongs and held grudges. It was like my senses had been hijacked and I was suddenly awakened to my surroundings and how haphazardly I had been dwelling in those surroundings. God had opened my eyes and awakened something in me that had long been asleep.

How can I adequately express my gratitude for this? I can't, really. But I can tell you that even in my joy of experiencing change, I was also disappointed that the changes were only happening in me. Yes, I was less offended by my husband's authoritative voice, but why was he still being harsh? I was more patient with my sons, but why were they still slow to respond to my requests? I was softening to strained relationships, but why was the relationship still strained? I had forgiven my abuser, but why wasn't he sorry? Why was I the only one changing?

Here I was, rejoicing in what God had done for me, and still it wasn't enough. I wanted God to change everyone around me too. Let's revisit Moses for a moment. Think about the Isrealites. God had freed them from slavery and was leading them to the promised land. While there's no doubt they were grateful for their newfound freedom, there's also no denying their selfish nature and incessant complaining. Read Exodus 16 with me:

> *Then all the Israelites left Elim. They reached the western Sinai desert, between Elim and Mount Sinai, on the fifteenth day of the second month after leaving Egypt. Then the whole community of Israelites began complaining again. They complained to Moses and Aaron in the desert. They said, "It would have been better if the Lord had just killed us in the land of Egypt. At least there we had plenty to eat. We had all the food we needed. But now you have brought us out here into this desert to make us all die from hunger."*

The Lord heard their complaints and gave them food. He caused flocks of quail to fill their camp at night and he gave them manna from heaven in the morning. What a gracious God we serve! The Israelites moved on and traveled as the Lord commanded, and what did they start doing again? Complaining.

> The Israelites left the western Sinai desert. They traveled all together from place to place as the Lord commanded. They camped at Rephidim, but there was no water for the people to drink. So they turned against Moses and started arguing with him. They said, "Give us water to drink."
>
> Moses said to them, "Why have you turned against me? Why are you testing the Lord?"
>
> But the people were very thirsty, so they continued complaining to Moses. They said, "Why did you bring us out of Egypt? Did you bring us out here so that we, our children, and our cattle will all die without water?"

We, in so many ways, are no different than the Israelites. We are a fickle people who are never satisfied. We complain when we don't get what we want when we want it and we aren't patient enough to wait and see what else God is going to do for us. Let me turn your attention to 1 Peter 3:1, which says, "Wives, in the same way, submit yourselves to your husbands, so that even if they refuse to believe the word, they will be won over without words by the behavior of their wives."

The reality of 1 Peter 3:1 became my reality in my marriage. My husband is a godly man - this wasn't about him not believing the Word. But the Lord used this verse to remind me that he brings about change in his own time. My "job" was to be faithful and to live out the change he was bringing about in me and to love, serve, and submit to my husband, and to trust that he too was being sanctified. All I could do was live out the lessons I was learning and trust that my husband would notice.

I am often reminded of how small my faith is, and this scenario is the perfect example. I wanted, from day one, for my husband to read the books I was reading, to attend the training conferences I was attending, and for his heart to be softened the way mine was. A day felt like a week, a week felt like a month. You get the picture - I was impatient. Here's what happened. My husband and I offer premarital and marital counseling to the members of our church family. During my training, as the Lord was bringing about change in me, Chad and I entered the counseling room together to pour into a young couple. Chad asked me to share some specific things I had been learning and when the session was over, my dear husband told me that he could see change in me. Growth. Not just as a counselor but as a wife, a mother, and as a daughter of the King. He complimented me, thanked me, praised God for the changes he saw and then . . . he said he wanted that for himself.

It was all in God's good timing. Had I nagged and had Chad read those books and attended those conferences just to appease me, we might have seen behavior modification, but over time I believe we would have also seen a division in our marriage. After all, Proverbs 21:9 says it's better to live on the corner of a roof than to share a house with a nagging wife. Ouch. Praise God that while I had this inner turmoil of wanting to nag, the Holy Spirit convicted me and prompted me to wait on the Lord. Waiting on the Lord is always the right answer. What's true for our counselees is true for us and those closest to us. Behavior modification is not what we want. We want heart change, and heart change doesn't come about from excessive nagging, but from the grace of God.

Chad has since started the training process, and every time we counsel together, we comment on how badly we wish we had had this training years ago. We think back to problems we had in our marriage early on and wish, so badly, that we had known what biblical counseling was so that we could have sought that out. We will often exchange examples of how we've counseled poorly in the past and how thankful we are for what we've learned. We point out changes in ourselves and in each other, give God glory for that, and look ahead with anticipation for the changes yet to come. The thought of getting better at what we do, at being better parents, better spouses, better sons and daughters, gives us such hope and excitement. And, looking back at how far we've come increases our faith and gives us confidence that the Lord will work in our counselees in his good time, just as he has done in us.

In his book *Perfect Sinners*, Matt Fuller talks about how our walk with the Lord fluctuates. He says, "Our walk with God changes regularly, perhaps on a daily basis (or even hourly). Our godliness is not constant; nor is our experience of God."[3] We have ups and downs. There are times when our faith is strong and we walk closely with the Lord, and there are times where our faith is weak and we take a step away from the Lord. I point this out because it's so important for us to remember that this is true for *all* of us. While I've spent time telling you about a season in life where I wanted to see more growth in my husband, I can also tell you about seasons where my husband wanted to see growth in me. I specifically remember when our sons (who are only nineteen months apart) were both in diapers. I was exhausted all the time, and what I chose to give up during that season of life was my Bible reading. Chad noticed this and began nagging me relentlessly. No, not really. There's not a verse that says it's better to live among the endless piles of laundry than to share a house with a nagging husband. Nagging isn't a go-to for men like it is for women. And praise God for that! So, what did Chad do? He encouraged me. When I was having an especially hard

---

[3] Matt Fuller, *Perfect Sinners: See Yourself as God Sees You* (United Kingdom: The Good Book Company, 2017), 9.

day and my attitude showed it, Chad would lovingly say, "Something that really helps me deal with bad days is being in the Word on a regular basis. If you could find time to make that happen for yourself, I bet you'd see it helped you too." And when I continued to neglect time in the Word, he didn't make me feel bad about it. He was patient. He waited for another natural opportunity to remind me of where real help, fuel and change comes from.

I never want to forget Matt Fuller's point, that *all* of our walks with the Lord fluctuate. We *all* experience seasons of growth just as we *all* experience seasons of being stagnant. So the next time we find ourselves wishing the people around us were growing, we need to remember that they've likely felt that way about us too. And if they haven't, I assure you God has. We need to be patient. We need to be long-suffering. We need to trust God's timing. We must remember that the only consistent thing in our lives, the only thing we can rely on to never need change, is God's love for us. Praise be to God!

Your specific circumstances might look different depending on your stage of life. For instance, if you're single, you might find yourself wanting your roommates, your best friend, or your coworkers to change. Maybe you work in ministry and, while your heart is being softened, you long to see the same in your co-laborers. Maybe you've devoted your retirement years to kingdom work, and you're disappointed in your friends who don't share the same drive and zeal. It's far too easy to exalt ourselves and judge those around us. It's far too easy to get tunnel vision, to see the path we're on, and assume those around us are simply sitting on the sidelines resting, ignoring the growth opportunities and staying stagnant in their sin. We are a judgmental people.

But God.

What's in your toolbox?

Friends, if you had a counselee come to you expressing disappointment or discouragement, what would you say to them? If you had a married woman come to you expressing frustration that her husband isn't growing or leading the way she wants him to, what would you say to her? I encourage you to visit the following scriptures in your Bible, for your counselee and for yourself.

1. Psalm 139:23-24

"Search me, O God, and know my heart! Try me and know my thoughts! And see if there be any grievous way in me, and lead me in the way everlasting!"

Consider these words from a dear friend of mine. "My mentor once said to me, 'Each morning, first thing, I pray two things: Father, thank you for another day of life, and Show me my heart.' Sometimes I find myself hesitant to pray that, because what he's going to show me, typically, is some big black smudge that I need to deal with. It took me a long time to understand that when he shows me the dark stains in my own heart, he's doing it from LOVE, not accusatory condemnation."

Ask God to search your heart. Ask him to see if your motives are right or wrong. Then ask God to allow his Spirit to convict you of any wrong thinking, selfish desires or any other grievous way he may find. Then ask him to lead you in the way everlasting!

2. Philippians 2:13

"For it is God who works in you, both to will and to work for his good pleasure."

We can want to see change come about in our loved ones all we want, but *we* can*not* bring about that change! We must submit to the sovereignty of God and wait for him to fulfill his purposes.

3. Isaiah 25:1

"O Lord, you are my God; I will exalt you; I will praise your name, for you have done wonderful things, plans formed of old, faithful and sure."

Remind yourself of the good works the Lord has done in you. How he's brought about change in you recently, and how he's brought about change over the entire course of your life. Remind yourself that he is faithful. Remind yourself that he has no desire to leave your loved ones in their sin. Trust that he is working in their lives and that change will come about in his perfect timing. Praise him! Praise him for the wonderful things he has done and for the wonderful things he has yet to do.

4. Psalm 22:5

"To you they cried and were rescued; in you they trusted and were not put to shame."

Another way of putting this is to say that they trusted in him and were not disappointed. Remind yourself that even though God doesn't desire to leave your loved ones in their sin, the change he brings about still might not be what you want it to be. We must trust not only in his perfect timing but in his sovereign will over our lives. When we trust him in all things, it is then, and only then, that we will not be disappointed.

5. Ecclesiastes 3:11

"He has made everything beautiful in its time. Also, he has put eternity into man's heart, yet so that he cannot find out what God has done from the beginning to the end."

Much of my sin boils down to not trusting God. Distrust is a root that I am always trying to pluck from the pit of my being. I find it exceedingly difficult to put one foot in front of the other not knowing where the path leads. But that's the thing - I do know. In those times between plucking out that destructive root and it growing back, I am able to see clearly. God's love and faithfulness are evident and for a time, until that root burrows down again, I can walk with confidence knowing it is the Lord who determines my steps. I know that God chose me to be his own. I know that Jesus bought me with his own blood. And I know that the Holy Spirit sealed me. We do not know what lies on the path between now and eternity, but we *do know* that our sovereign God holds our times in his hands, and we can trust that he has made everything beautiful in its time.

6. Romans 15:1-2

"We who are strong have an obligation to bear with the failings of the weak, and not to please ourselves. Let each of us please his neighbor for his good, to build him up."

Whether we have legitimate concerns about the growth of those around us or not, we are not told to be frustrated, to be bitter, to be annoyed or to be disappointed. We aren't told that we have an obligation to sit and stew while we wait for everyone else to grow and change. No, we're told we have an obligation to bear with the failings of the weak. To please them for their good. To build them up. And guess what? Fulfilling this obligation is part of our sanctification, part of our growth, part of bringing about change in us. While we like to think of ourselves as the strong ones, we too are weak. We all have failings and need to be built up.

7. 1 Peter 5:7-9

"Casting all your anxieties on him, because he cares for you. Be sober-minded; be watchful. Your adversary the devil prowls around like a roaring lion, seeking someone to devour. Resist him, firm in your faith, knowing that the same kinds of suffering are being experienced by your brotherhood throughout the world."

The enemy wants you to be discouraged. He wants you to be annoyed with your spouse or your kids or your coworkers. He wants you to be discontented with their attitudes. He wants you to question the Lord's goodness and more than anything, he wants you to distrust God. Yet, your Heavenly Father cares for you and invites you not only to lay your discouragement at his feet, but to find encouragement in him! By the power of the Holy Spirit you can avoid giving in to bitterness or frustration toward those around you. As Matt Fuller says, "We should long to change but not despair that change takes time."[4] Stand firm in your faith! Look to Jesus, and fully rely on him. Trust him in all things, including his timing, because he cares for you.

---

[4] Fuller, *Perfect Sinners,* 10.

Encouragement

This chapter is entitled "I'm changing, why aren't you?" While I'm addressing this from the perspective of my own sinful heart, I want to point out that you might ask this question and it *not* stem from a sinful heart. For instance, it's good to want the people in our lives to be sanctified and to look more like Jesus! I don't want my husband to be content with how I am, I want him to spur me on to be more Christ-like, and I think he would say the same.

It's possible that the Lord has opened the eyes of your heart, brought you to himself, and led you down the path to biblical counseling while your spouse has yet to be reborn. Or, perhaps you're single and your inner circle of friends lacks a saving faith. It's right for you to want them to change. It's right for you to call out to the Lord and beg for their salvation. So, whether you relate to me and my selfish nature, or to those who desperately want someone they love to have the eyes of their hearts opened, there is hope. There is encouragement.

- **He invites us to cast our cares on him.**

Philippians 4:6-7 tells us, "Do not be anxious about anything, but in everything by prayer and supplication with thanksgiving let your requests be made known to God. And the peace of God, which surpasses all understanding, will guard your hearts and your minds in Christ Jesus."

When we cast our cares on him, when we ask him to bring about change in those we love, and when we spend time thanking him for his faithfulness and his mercies, his peace will guard our hearts and our minds. His peace, which passes all understanding, will help us to rest in him, trust in him and wait for his perfect timing.

- **He is good!**

Daniel 9:18 reminds us that "We do not make requests of you because we are righteous, but because of your great mercy."

I can't think of anything more *dis*couraging than to think that God only hears our prayers if we've done enough, if we're good enough or if we've changed enough. No, we go to God with anticipation of his answering our prayers because of *his* great mercy. I pray this truth will encourage you all the days of your life.

- **He desires not just that *we* change, but our loved ones too.**

2 Peter 3:9 says, "The Lord is not slow to fulfill his promise as some count slowness, but is patient toward you, not wishing that any should perish, but that all should reach repentance."

When you feel like you're the only one who is growing and the only one who is changing, remind yourself of this truth. God is patient with your loved ones just as he was patient with you. God wishes no man to perish, but that all should reach repentance. This gives us such an intimate look into God's character and his love for us. Don't be dismayed. Be patient. Trust him.

Personal Reflection

1.   What are some ways God has changed you through your training as a biblical counselor?

2.   Write about a time when you saw change in yourself and desired to see change in those around you.

3.   What do you think those desires stemmed from?

4.   Write about a time when someone in your life desired to see change in you.

5.   How did the Lord bring about that change?

6.   How would you encourage a counselee who was impatient about the Lord bringing about change in either themselves or in the life of someone they love?

Chapter 3

When Dread Sets In

Only those who try to resist temptation know how strong it is...We never find out the strength of the evil impulse inside us until we try to fight it.

C.S. Lewis, *Mere Christianity*

We started homeschooling our sons when they were in early elementary school. I can still remember the day we sat down to tell the boys about our big decision. My husband and I are both planners, so we called the boys into the living room with our dry erase board set up, ready to display our pros and cons. We had prepared a talk that was sure to convince anyone that homeschooling was the way to go. Our boys, who at the time were going into the 2nd and 3rd grades, came into the living room and surveyed the scene. The dry erase board was set up, mom and dad both had papers in their hands. This was serious. In fact, this might have been the first family meeting we had ever called in their young lives. My heart was beating out of my chest while Chad had calmly transitioned into businessman mode, ready to sell a valuable product to a reluctant customer. I remember our boys looking curious, but also a little anxious.

Chad and I had spent weeks praying that the Lord would prepare their little hearts for this conversation, that they wouldn't argue or protest. After all, our boys had no real complaints about public school. I remember Chad calmly started our family meeting and simply told the boys that after much prayer and consideration, we had come to the conclusion that we wanted to pull them out of public school and educate them at home. I'm not sure about Chad, but I held my breath waiting for their response. I mean, kids at that age just say the first thing that pops into their heads, and there's often no rhyme or reason to it. Hence our preparations to respond to any possible objection and to answer any possible question. But here's the thing. Our little boys, in unison, simply exclaimed, "Thank you!"

That summer Chad and I attended our first homeschooling conference. I excitedly picked out the curriculum, bought a special bookcase for all our books, wrote out our daily schedule - remember, I'm a planner. I was on cloud nine! Day One rolled around and the boys and I had a blast. We all three felt so accomplished in our own ways. Our day was filled with conversation and laughter. We snuggled under a blanket and read a book together, and the worksheets - the glorious worksheets! The circling, the underlining, and filling in the blanks - their enjoyment of this proved they're our children. I went to bed that night praising God for what a great day we had had and I felt blessed beyond measure. But then I woke up the next morning and it hit me. I had to do it all again that day, and the next, and the next. Suddenly all that joy and excitement dissipated and I found myself full of dread. What were we thinking? What on earth qualified me to educate our boys? I didn't want to get out of bed. I wanted the night to continue with me snuggled down under the covers, hiding.

This, my friends, is how I felt in the early days of counseling. And if I'm being honest, this is sometimes how I feel even now. I've felt this with the dream counselee, you know the one. You've introduced yourself, they tell you why they've come and all the while you're thinking to yourself, "I could be friends with this person." You get a clear vision of what they're struggling with and you even start mentally laying out a plan for them. You have complete confidence that God's Word can speak to their issues and that the Holy Spirit will do the work. The session ends with both of you smiling, both of you feeling hopeful, and both of you looking forward to your next session. Why on earth would anyone dread this?

It's easier to understand dreading the hard cases, right? Your counselee enters the session with tears in her eyes, you tell a bit about yourself to put them at ease, but you can tell they're not really listening, they just want to get to the point so that you can fix their problems. They finally tell you why they're seeking help, and the more they talk the more inadequate you feel. You watch their mouth move but you've almost stopped listening because you're praying for wisdom. You trust God, but can he *really* help this person? You point, with faltering confidence, to the Word and offer the hope that only comes from our heavenly Father. The session ends with you both looking downcast, both feeling overwhelmed, and you schedule the next session trying not to look like a deer in the headlights.

Easy case or hard case, you spend the week following your regular routine. You're in the Word, you spend time in prayer for your counselees, you spend some time preparing for your next sessions, and you look ahead with great anticipation to see what God will do. You love being a counselor! You go to bed the night before praying for a good night's sleep, for compassion, for patience, and for wisdom while administering God's Word. You close your eyes thinking of how faithful God is and how humbled you are that he would see fit to use you in this way. You feel love, you feel gratitude, and you drift off to sleep knowing you are kept by the I AM.

Your alarm clock goes off the following morning. Maybe you're like me and you hit snooze once, twice, three times . . . and then once more for good measure. Or, maybe you're one of those morning people who got some kind of special tonic when you were born that allows you to jump right out of bed and face the day as if the sound of the alarm clock is itself a dose of caffeine. Yawning or smiling, you're ready to start the day. Until you realize what day it is. It's counseling day. And suddenly you feel a tingling rush through your body, your head feels fuzzy and you wonder for a split second if you're getting sick, so maybe you should cancel on everyone. After all, it's not kind to spread germs. While brushing your teeth you realize you're not sick, but this realization comes with a bit of disappointment. It's one of the few times in life you actually wish you were sick. You face yourself in the mirror and all you can do is ask yourself, "Why, why did I think I could do this?"

Let me get one thing straight. My dread over homeschooling day after day had nothing to do with my love, commitment, or servanthood to my children. In the same way, my dread over counseling has nothing to do with my love, commitment, or servanthood to my counselees. The dread comes from two sources: the enemy and my flesh. I don't always recognize this in the moment. Sometimes it takes a few minutes of me swallowing hard to confirm if my throat really is sore or not. But once I do recognize what's happening, I immediately think of Eve in the garden of Eden. Recall Genesis 3:1 with me.

> *Now the serpent was more crafty than any other beast of the field that the Lord God had made. He said to the woman, "Did God actually say, 'You shall not eat of any tree in the garden'?"*

Oh, the power of that one little question, "Did God actually say . . .?" The enemy knows the power of doubt and how easily persuaded we are. When I first started homeschooling, I found myself fighting questions like, "Are you really smart enough to teach your children? Aren't there other things you would rather be doing? Did you actually pray about this?" You get the idea. With my counselees I fight questions like, "Are you really wise enough to counsel someone? What if you make their problems worse? Did God really say his grace is sufficient? Don't you have your own issues to work on?"

In Exodus chapter 3 we find God making plans to free the Israelites from the Egyptians. God instructs Moses on how to address Pharoah, and I find myself relating to Moses' response. Let's pick up the narrative in verse 9 as God says:

> *"And now, behold, the cry of the people of Israel has come to me, and I have also seen the oppression with which the Egyptians oppress them. Come, I will send you to Pharaoh that you may bring my people, the children of Israel, out of Egypt." But Moses said to God, "Who am I that I should go to Pharaoh and bring the children of Israel out of Egypt?" He said, "But I will be with you, and this shall be the sign for you, that I have sent you: when you have brought the people out of Egypt, you shall serve God on this mountain."*

This is the exact question I find myself asking: "Who am *I* to do this thing?"

Moses is busy formulating his next question, followed by God's amazing response:

> *Then Moses said to God, "If I come to the people of Israel and say to them, 'The God of your fathers has sent me to you,' and they ask me, 'What is his name?' what shall I say to them?" God said to Moses, "I AM WHO I AM." And he said, "Say this to the people of Israel: 'I AM has sent me to you.'"* (3:13-14)

I think Moses and I were cut from the same cloth that all planners are cut from, because I too would have asked, "But if they ask this, what do I say?"

God goes on to give Moses very specific instructions to gather the elders of Israel, to tell them that God has appeared to him, to repeat his words and then together they will go to the king of Egypt. I'm not surprised by Moses' response in 4:1.

> *Then Moses answered, "But behold, they will not believe me or listen to my voice, for they will say, 'The Lord did not appear to you.'"*

God is so patient. At this point, as a parent, my anger would have surfaced and the scene would have taken a turn for the worse. But God is the perfect parent that I will never be. He has an important object lesson for his reluctant servant:

> *The Lord said to him, "What is that in your hand?" He said, "A staff." And he said, "Throw it on the ground." So he threw it on the ground, and it became a serpent, and Moses ran from it. But the Lord said to Moses, "Put out your hand and catch it by the tail"—so he put out his hand and caught it, and it became a staff in his hand— "that they may believe that the Lord, the God of their fathers, the God of Abraham, the God of Isaac, and the God of Jacob, has appeared to you." Again, the Lord said to him, "Put your hand inside your cloak." And he put his hand inside his cloak, and when he took it out, behold, his hand was leprous like snow. Then God said, "Put your hand back inside your cloak." So he put his hand back inside his cloak, and when he took it out, behold, it was restored like the rest of his flesh. "If*

they will not believe you," God said, "or listen to the first sign,
they may believe the latter sign. If they will not believe even these
two signs or listen to your voice, you shall take some water from
the Nile and pour it on the dry ground, and the water that you
shall take from the Nile will become blood on the dry ground."
(4:2-9)

Okay, at this point I'm not sure how I would have reacted, but again, probably something like Moses: overlooking what God is doing and focusing on myself.

But Moses said to the Lord, "Oh, my Lord, I am not eloquent,
either in the past or since you have spoken to your servant, but I
am slow of speech and of tongue." Then the Lord said to him,
"Who has made man's mouth? Who makes him mute, or deaf, or
seeing, or blind? Is it not I, the Lord? Now therefore go, and I
will be with your mouth and teach you what you shall speak." But
he said, "Oh, my Lord, please send someone else." (4:10-13)

I'm always amazed that it took so long for the anger of the Lord to be kindled against Moses. But even in his anger, God was so gracious. He could have struck Moses down. He could have made him mute. He could have responded with a myriad of questions like he did with Job. But instead, God gave him Aaron.

Then the anger of the Lord was kindled against Moses and he
said, "Is there not Aaron, your brother, the Levite? I know that
he can speak well. Behold, he is coming out to meet you, and when
he sees you, he will be glad in his heart. You shall speak to him
and put the words in his mouth, and I will be with your mouth
and with his mouth and will teach you both what to do. He shall
speak for you to the people, and he shall be your mouth, and you

shall be as God to him. And take in your hand this staff, with which you shall do the signs." (4:14-17)

I think this account of Moses and Aaron comes to mind because this is exactly what I face. When I find myself questioning my ability to do anything, but especially counsel someone, I find myself overlooking God's power and his proven faithfulness. I get stuck focusing on myself and on my inadequacies. It's then that I hear those questions sneaking in, "Are you really good enough to do this? Did God really lead you down this path? Is God really pleased with how you're handling his word?" And then I do exactly what Moses did. I find myself asking God, "Wouldn't you rather use someone else? I'm not eloquent."

This is typically when I run to my husband Chad and tell him I think I need to stop counseling. This is when Chad, faithfully, reminds me that I'm believing lies and listening to the wrong voices. He reminds me that yes, I've had some not-so-great counseling sessions. I've messed up and I'll continue to mess up. But God is always faithful and he never makes mistakes. Chad reminds me of the amazing work the Holy Spirit has done in some of my counselees and how I can take the pressure off myself to be good enough. Because I'm not good enough. I'm not eloquent. I am, however, a child of God and I serve the same King Jesus who told his disciples not to be anxious about defending themselves when brought before the synagogues and rulers and authorities. Jesus told them that the Holy Spirit would teach them in that very hour what they ought to say (see Luke 12:11-12). This is where my confidence comes from, trusting in the work of the Holy Spirit, not myself. This is where, I pray, you find your confidence too.

Refocusing on these truths will calm me down for a bit. In fact, it's after these conversations with my husband that I find myself in prayer praising God for his faithfulness, his love and sovereignty over our lives. But I have to admit, this is where the other source of my dread sneaks in. My flesh. Something I'm reminded of daily is that even though I have been cleansed by the blood of Jesus Christ, I remain susceptible to carnal desires and continue to yearn for earthly satisfaction. In short, I'm selfish.

I can speak truth to myself and spend the entire morning worshiping the Lord, but the instant I take my focus off of him, my focus turns back to myself. I'm not sick, we've established that. I know I'm believing lies and listening to the wrong voices. Okay, got it. Refocus on the Lord and his goodness. Check. Oh how I wish it stopped there. But what happens next is that I start thinking of all the other things I could be doing if I weren't counseling. There's the logical stuff, the stuff that seems justified, like dishes and laundry. Might I be honoring God more by simply serving my family? Shouldn't I be at the supermarket today getting groceries for the week?

Then there's the less justifiable, more selfish stuff. I could be working on my next book. I could be reading. After all, I can't be a good counselor if I'm not reading books on the subject (mind you, if I gave in to this I would likely pick up a fiction novel to momentarily escape reality). I could be shopping. Don't I deserve a day to myself to relax and focus on *my* mental health? Honestly, the list goes on and on. My flesh is never lacking for reasons to ignore everyone else in my life and do what will make me happy instead. Paul comes to mind in times like these.

> *For I do not understand my own actions. For I do not do what I want, but I do the very thing I hate. Now if I do what I do not want, I agree with the law, that it is good. So now it is no longer I who do it, but sin that dwells within me. For I know that nothing good dwells in me, that is, in my flesh. For I have the desire to do what is right, but not the ability to carry it out. For I do not do the good I want, but the evil I do not want is what I keep on*

doing. Now if I do what I do not want, it is no longer I who do it, but sin that dwells within me. (Romans 7:15-20)

Am I the only one who will have plenty to talk to Paul about in the hereafter? Let's keep reading.

> *So I find it to be a law that when I want to do right, evil lies close at hand. For I delight in the law of God, in my inner being, but I see in my members another law waging war against the law of my mind and making me captive to the law of sin that dwells in my members. Wretched man that I am! Who will deliver me from this body of death? Thanks be to God through Jesus Christ our Lord! So then, I myself serve the law of God with my mind, but with my flesh I serve the law of sin."* (7:21-25)

I have to admit, this is all difficult for me to write. I don't like putting my sin on display. I don't want anyone to know that I sometimes dread facing my counselees. I want everyone to assume I wake up wishing everyday were counseling day. I want all of you to look at me and see a contagious passion for serving others. However, writing all of that would make me a liar. I'm willing to display my sin because I know I'm not the only one. In fact, we are all - each and every one of us - very much in the same boat. We are all passengers on the SS Sinful Nature and as it sinks from our weight, we all rely on the same life preserver: Jesus Christ. And because of *HIM* we can follow Paul into Romans chapter 8, fall to our knees, and praise him.

> *There is therefore now no condemnation for those who are in Christ Jesus. For the law of the Spirit of life has set you free in Christ Jesus from the law of sin and death. For God has done what the law, weakened by the flesh, could not do. By sending his own Son in the likeness of sinful flesh and for sin, he condemned sin in the flesh, in order that the righteous requirement of the law*

might be fulfilled in us, who walk not according to the flesh but according to the Spirit. (Romans 8:1-4)

This makes me want to exclaim, "Amen!" But wait, there's more.

For those who live according to the flesh set their minds on the things of the flesh, but those who live according to the Spirit set their minds on the things of the Spirit. For to set the mind on the flesh is death, but to set the mind on the Spirit is life and peace. For the mind that is set on the flesh is hostile to God, for it does not submit to God's law; indeed, it cannot. Those who are in the flesh cannot please God. (8:5-8)

Wait for it.

You, however, are not in the flesh but in the Spirit, if in fact the Spirit of God dwells in you. *Anyone who does not have the Spirit of Christ does not belong to him. But if Christ is in you, although the body is dead because of sin, the Spirit is life because of righteousness. If the Spirit of him who raised Jesus from the dead dwells in you, he who raised Christ Jesus from the dead will also give life to your mortal bodies through his Spirit who dwells in you.* (8:9-11)

When Chris Tomlin added "My Chains Are Gone" to Amazing Grace, I thought, "What has this guy done?" But as I sang those words, I got it.

My chains are gone
I've been set free
My God, my Savior has ransomed me
And like a flood His mercy reigns
Unending love, amazing grace[5]

---

[5] Chris Tomlin, "Amazing Grace (My Chains Are Gone)," 2006, track 11 on *See the Morning*, Six Step Records, compact disc.

What Romans tells us is that because of Jesus Christ, we are no longer slaves to sin. We no longer live in the flesh, but in the Spirit. Our chains are gone! We don't have to listen when our flesh tells us that we could or should be doing something else. We have answers when the enemy prods us with questions and tries to fill our minds with doubt. Here's the thing: sin will get us every time. If I listen to the enemy, I start doubting not only my abilities as a counselor but also God's goodness. That leads me to doubt that God ever wanted me to be a counselor as well as to doubt that his Word is sufficient. If I listen to my flesh, I convince myself that the counselee would be better off without me and I would be better off to go do the things *I* want to do.

The conflict here, between my spirit and my flesh, is that I *do* want to counsel. I *do* want to serve others. I *do* want to utilize God's Word and point others to his everlasting love. But my sinful nature makes it all too easy to want other things more. To take the easy way out. When I stop and think about this struggle, I become so disgusted with my sin that I'm tempted to just throw in the towel, crawl back in bed and let the minutes tick on without me. This struggle reminds me of a quotation from Martin Luther:

> *So when the devil throws your sins in your face and declares that you deserve death and hell, tell him this: "I admit that I deserve death and hell, what of it? For I know One who suffered and made satisfaction on my behalf. His name is Jesus Christ, Son of God, and where He is there I shall be also!"*[6]

I keep Luther's wise words at the forefront of my mind because this is the attitude I strive for. In those moments when the accuser has me

---

[6] Martin Luther, *Letters of Spiritual Counsel,* trans. and ed. Theodore G. Tappert (Vancouver, British Columbia: Regent College, 2003), 86-87.

right where he wants me, in that mindset of self condemnation, I need the reminder to stand up straight and say, "Yes. It's true. I'm not the best counselor. I am selfish. I am sinful. Sinful to my core, in fact. But, I have been bought with a price. My chains are gone. I am no longer a slave to that sin that heckles me. I can move forward, by faith. I can face my counselees with no need of self-confidence because my confidence lies in the One, and only One, who can bring about change."

This, my friends, is where we draw the strength and courage to continue entering the counseling room. Not with fear of our own shortcomings, but with full confidence in God and in his Word. We should not only put off our own selfishness, but then put on the armor of God so that we can fight with and for our counselees. We should not be afraid of the accusations the enemy hurls at us, because with the shield of faith we can extinguish those flaming darts. We should make sure our belt of truth is securely fastened, and if there is any sin we need to confess, know that the Lord will reveal it to us. By putting on the breastplate of righteousness, we are clothed with the Lord Jesus himself. Thus armed by these and the other pieces of armor at our disposal, we are able to stand firm, and by the power of the Holy Spirit, to go and serve those whom the Lord has entrusted to us.

What's in Your Toolbox?

It's important to remember that we can apply almost anything we experience as counselors to the lives of our counselees. Perhaps you have a counselee who dreads going to work every morning or dreads going home at the end of the day and facing his or her spouse. Perhaps you're working with a pregnant woman who dreads caring for another child. Maybe your counselee dreads the long term effects of a recent diagnosis. The scenarios are endless, but it's a reality that we all experience dread, that deep-seated reluctance and anxiety to face a person or situation.

Just as we would say to a counselee, we as counselors need to be honest about where our dread is coming from. What is the root that grows into dread? The specific tool you use will depend on the root that needs plucked. The following tools will help move you in the right direction.

1.   2 Corinthians 10:5

"We destroy arguments and every lofty opinion raised against the knowledge of God, and take every thought captive to obey Christ."

When dread sets in, for any reason, remember there is hope to be found in 2 Corinthians 10:5. We know that God, in his lovingkindness, has promised to give us a way out of temptation and one of those ways is by taking our thoughts captive. Just as Paul, by the power of the Holy Spirit, used the Word to destroy the false, philosophical ideas of those in Corinth, we also must also ask the Spirit to reveal our false thinking about God and about ourselves. We should surrender our false thinking and allow the Spirit not only to redirect our thoughts away from falsehood, but also bring our thoughts into conformity with Christ.

2. Philippians 4:8-9

"Finally, brothers, whatever is true, whatever is honorable, whatever is just, whatever is pure, whatever is lovely, whatever is commendable, if there is any excellence, if there is anything worthy of praise, think about these things. What you have learned and received and heard and seen in me—practice these things, and the God of peace will be with you."

In the moment, when dread seems to be the very fiber that's holding you together, God's peace is the farthest thing from your mind. But as you make a habit of taking your thoughts captive, you will become more aware of your need for the peace of God. Philippians 4:8-9 gives you the perfect outline for redirecting your thoughts to things that will lift you up and away from the dread that weighs you down. In short, redirect your thoughts to Jesus.

3. Proverbs 3:5-6

"Trust in the Lord with all your heart, and do not lean on your own understanding. In all your ways acknowledge him, and he will make straight your paths."

There may be times when you can't pinpoint why you're filled with dread. It isn't always obvious. These are the times when it's especially important to trust in the Lord and not on your own understanding. Because our own hearts are deceitful, you can't allow your feelings to dictate your decision making. You can trust the Lord to make your paths straight. You can trust him to free you from the dread that is keeping you from serving with joy.

4. Hebrews 13:20-21

"Now may the God of peace who brought again from the dead our Lord Jesus, the great shepherd of the sheep, by the blood of the eternal covenant, equip you with everything good that you may do his will, working in us that which is pleasing in his sight, through Jesus Christ, to whom be glory forever and ever. Amen."

If your dread is being fueled by lies from the enemy, direct your thoughts to Hebrews 13:20-21. If God has led you to be a biblical counselor, he will not leave you ill-equipped for the task. He not only cares for you, but he cares for your counselee. You can trust that he will equip you with everything good that you may do his will.

5. Philippians 2:3-4

"Do nothing from selfish ambition or conceit, but in humility count others more significant than yourselves. Let each of you look not only to his own interests, but also to the interests of others."

Biblical counseling is often a thankless job, which makes it easier for us to be tempted by our selfish desires. We can easily convince ourselves that we deserve a break, a day off, a day of personal pleasure. But when we set our minds to God's great love for us, for Jesus' mind-blowing sacrifice for us, we can joyfully put our selfish desires aside and serve the Lord by serving our counselees.

6. 2 Timothy 3:16-17

"All Scripture is breathed out by God and profitable for teaching, for reproof, for correction, and for training in righteousness, that the man of God may be complete, equipped for every good work."

Does the enemy distract you with doubt? He does me. It's in those moments that we can cling to 2 Timothy and know that our knowledge, our words, our thoughts and opinions aren't what we're taking into the counseling room. We can enter the counseling room with full confidence knowing we are armed with God's word and through his word we are equipped for every good work.

7. James 4:7

"Submit yourselves therefore to God. Resist the devil, and he will flee from you."

This reminds me of Jesus being tempted in the wilderness. How did Jesus resist the devil? He quoted scripture! This reminds me of the responsibility we have, not just as biblical counselors, but as children of God, to store up his word in our hearts so that we might not sin against him. Stay in the Word, store his truths in your heart, submit to God. Making this a lifelong habit will help us face the counseling day, and everyday, with less dread and more joy.

Friends, the enemy wants to distract us. He doesn't want us walking into the counseling room with confidence in God's Word. He wants more than anything for us to be filled with dread. It's important for us to remember that we, as biblical counselors, are not immune to the devil's schemes. If anything, we are more susceptible because he doesn't want God to use us. He doesn't want God to bring about change.

Before I sat down to finish writing this chapter, I read day 8 in David Dunham's *Addictive Habits: Changing For Good*. This is a daily devotional that I am currently reading with a friend. As I read day 8, I couldn't help but smile at how God consistently uses resources for more than one purpose. I'd like to share a bit of Dunham's thoughts with you. He is speaking specifically to Philippians 4:8 "Finally, brothers, whatever is true, whatever is honorable, whatever is just, whatever is pure, whatever is lovely, whatever is commendable, if there is any excellence, if there is anything worthy of praise, think about these things." Dunham says,

> *Change does not come simply from mentally assenting to "these things." It comes from serious, deep meditation and reflection on these commendable qualities. We need to wrestle with what is "true" and calculate in our minds whatever things are "lovely."*

> *Dwelling on "these things" means moving them from abstraction to specifics. Certainly we should focus on these things as they apply to life in general. It's easy to focus on everything wrong in life and to miss all the lovely and excellent things. But ultimately the point of the passage is to fix our minds on that which is the epitome of all these things: Jesus. Each of these items finds its ultimate expression in Jesus.*

> *So who is true? Jesus (see John 1:17; 14:6). Who is honorable? Jesus (see John 5:23). Who is just? Jesus (see Rev. 15:3). Who is pure? Jesus (see 1 John 3:3). Who is lovely? Jesus (see Ps. 45:2). Who is commendable? Jesus (see Rev. 5:12). Who is excellent? Jesus (see Hebrews 1:4). Who is worthy of praise? Jesus (see Heb.*

3:3; Reb 4:11; 5:9, 12). We must fix our minds on Jesus; he is the true realization of all these qualities."[7]

When you find yourselves facing the day with dread, direct your mind and heart towards Jesus, as he has set you free from the bondage of sin. Your Heavenly Father will equip you to do his will and therefore you, and I, can face our counselees with full confidence in him. Praise be to God!

---

[7] David R. Dunham, *Addictive Habits: Changing for Good (31-Day Devotionals for Life)* (Phillipsburg, New Jersey: P & R Publishing Company, 2018), 31-32.

Encouragement

My hope in sharing this dread I sometimes feel is that you will know you're not alone. Your dread might look different than mine. The lies the enemy feeds you and the temptations of your flesh might not look the same as mine. But one thing I know to be true is that we are all in a fight against our sinful nature and our only hope is Christ, the One who suffered and made satisfaction on our behalf.

- **You're not the only one.**

1 Corinthians 10:13 says, *"No temptation has overtaken you that is not common to man."*

Whatever it is that steals your joy in the counseling room, fills you with dread, or convinces you that God's Word is not trustworthy, you are not the only one to fight against that "it". In those moments when you feel numb, or you're fluttering with anxiety, or you're experiencing any number of the emotions in between, remind yourself that,

"God is faithful, and he will not let you be tempted beyond your ability, but with the temptation he will also provide the way of escape, that you may be able to endure it."

- **You have nothing to fear.**

Psalm 27:1 says, *"The Lord is my light and my salvation; whom shall I fear? The Lord is the stronghold of my life; of whom shall I be afraid?"*

If you're like me, dread is often accompanied by fear. Fear that the lies I'm believing are true. Fear that I can't overcome the desires of my flesh. Fear that God is unhappy with me. Fear that I'm not enough. But, we don't have to be afraid of any of those things! We know who we are and whose we are. We know the Lord is our light and salvation. He is the stronghold of our lives and we have nothing and no one to fear.

- **You are not a slave to sin!**

Romans 6:14 says, *"For sin will have no dominion over you, since you are not under law but under grace."*

I'm a fairly somber, melancholy person. I rarely raise my hands in worship and if I've ever said "Amen" during a sermon it was a whisper. But, when I read these words in Romans, let's just say there's a party going on inside my heart. A party with lots of dancing, hand raising, bowing, kneeling, fist pumping, shouts of acclamation and praise! How do you respond to this truth? What emotions do these verses conjure up in you?

But thanks be to God, that you who were once slaves of sin have become obedient from the heart to the standard of teaching to which you were committed, and, having been set free from sin, have become slaves of righteousness. I am speaking in human terms, because of your natural limitations. For just as you once presented your members as slaves to impurity and to lawlessness leading to more lawlessness, so now present your members as slaves to righteousness leading to sanctification." (6:17-19)

Personal Reflections

1.   What is an example of a time you felt dread before facing a counselee? Where do you think that dread stems from?

2.   What lies from the enemy do you tend to believe about yourself and/or about God?

3.   What are some ways you are being distracted by fleshly desires? What are some ways you can combat these distractions?

4.   What are some scriptures you find helpful when anxious thoughts pile up inside you?

5.   Ask the Lord to reveal any patterns of dread in your life. What steps can you take to rid your life of those patterns?

6.   What changes do you need to make in your thinking or daily habits to refocus your thoughts on Jesus?

Chapter 4

When expectations aren't met

Every day in a life fills the whole life with expectations and memory.
C.S. Lewis, *Out of the Silent Planet*

Carol called on a Saturday afternoon. When I answered the phone she asked if she was talking to Beth Baus, the biblical counselor. I answered "Yes" and then sat silent for the next several minutes while she told me what was troubling her. When she was finally done, she took a deep breath and quickly added, "I need a counselor who won't have any personal issues that will ever take precedence over me and my needs."

I gently explained to Carol that finding a counselor without any personal issues would likely be impossible. I'm not exactly sure what issues Carol was imagining, but a few scenarios went through my mind. Friends of ours, a married couple who offer biblical counseling, recently had to take time off to be with their daughter during a cancer diagnosis and surgery. An older female counselor recently told me she takes time off every winter to go to Florida. I know of others who take a month off every year to refocus and rest. Life happens. Sickness interferes. Vacations intrude. The need for rest disrupts one's routine. While these are not all "issues" as Carol put it, they are all personal reasons that *will* supersede the counselee. Even though I knew Carol's expectations were unreasonably high, I felt bad knowing I couldn't meet them.

Have you ever felt bad for not meeting the expectations of a counselee? Or your own expectations for that matter? I deal with this on a regular basis. Let me tell you a bit about my broken body. I have psoriatic arthritis, which means I live with chronic pain and fatigue. The pain I experience is unpredictable. Sometimes I'll get a stabbing pain in the bottom of my foot, a few minutes later it might feel like I hit my elbow on a sharp edge, an hour later my hip might throb like a toothache and then my upper back will start burning like it's on fire. In other words, the pain moves around and there's no rhyme or reason to the severity of pain or how long it lasts. Last year I had several months where my tailbone hurt so bad I had to carry around an orthopedic pillow. This hadn't been embarrassing to me until a young woman at church asked rather loudly, "Is that one of those hemorrhoid pillows?" I did a lot of deep sighing that day.

My current battle is with my right jaw. This week I met my counselees hoping they wouldn't notice my teeth weren't lined up and that I couldn't close my mouth all the way without gasping in pain. This was also a week that I didn't take many notes in my sessions. My wrist was aching and my hand felt too weak to grasp the pen. I often get what is called "jello syndrome," where my arms feel weak and wobbly like a bowl of jello. When this happens my grip isn't tight and I drop things easily. Sometimes I push through and take notes anyway, but then of course I can't read my own writing when I go back to reference the session, so I have to ask, what's the point?

Psoriatic arthritis is considered an autoimmune disease, and thus I am more susceptible to illness. My rheumatologist described it like this, "Imagine your body is the United States of America. Imagine your arthritis is a terrorist group and your immune system is the United States Army. In a perfect world, the United States Army would fight to protect the USA from the terrorist group. But, in your case, the United States Army is working *with* the terrorist group to destroy the USA." That's a lovely image, isn't it?

When I have a flare-up, meaning an undetermined period of time when I have increased disease activity and worsening symptoms, my normal routine is forced to change. For me a flare-up is not only heightened pain and fatigue, but I will often have flu-like symptoms including body aches, chills, headaches, a sore throat and digestive issues. I also experience brain fog which makes concentration difficult. On a normal day I wake up feeling tired and fight fatigue throughout the day. But during a flare-up, I can wake up from a full night's sleep and feel like I haven't slept at all. There's no pushing through and naps are a must. It's during these times that I have no choice but to cancel my counseling sessions.

Thankfully, so far, my counselees have been understanding. Even if they're disappointed, they are still kind, for which I am exceedingly grateful. But I can't help thinking about Carol. For a multitude of reasons, I helped her find another counselor who was more suited to her specific needs. But I know that had I taken her on as a counselee, my own needs would have inevitably taken precedence over hers. Her bluntness about the matter makes me wonder how my other counselees really feel when I have to cancel on them. And I admit, this is when I get discouraged about the broken body I live in and I get disappointed in the fact that I physically can't do all the things I want to do.

When I first felt the nudge to be certified as a biblical counselor, I honestly wondered how this would work. After all, my doctor had told me I shouldn't work outside the home if possible. In fact, I was told to lie down for 10-15 minutes after every 1 -2 hours of activity. So, here I am. My earthly body is broken and doesn't meet my expectations. Yet, I want to serve the Lord and he has opened doors for me to pursue counseling. What this means for me is that I have to be mindful of my limitations and plan accordingly. Where other counselors I know start sessions at 8 am (sometimes earlier), I don't start til 10. Although I have a space available to me at our church office, I conduct counseling sessions in my home. I make exceptions to this rule when necessary, but it's best for me to have the option of resting between sessions and having easy access to things like heating pads and my orthopedic pillow.

I fear I've painted a picture of an elderly woman, hunched over, shuffling from room to room with twisted arthritic fingers. As I write this I am in my mid-forties. I stand up straight and though I have an occasional limp, my fingers aren't twisted – yet. I look healthy. Only my closest friends and family know the extent of my daily struggle. I do ask for prayer from time to time but generally speaking, I don't talk about it much. This creates a situation where people stare when my mom, who is in her mid-seventies, is pushing the overloaded grocery cart instead of me. She will often laugh and say, "Let them stare, maybe they'll just think I'm old and off balance and the cart is keeping me up." But the truth is, there are days when my mom's arms are stronger than mine and she almost always has more energy than I do. This, the fact that you can't see what's going on inside my body, creates a fear in me that my counselees think I'm exaggerating when I have to cancel due to my health, adding to my fear of not meeting their expectations.

Unmet expectations are all around us. We find them in marriage, in singleness, parenting and friendships, the workplace and in our church families. We don't always meet the expectations of our counselees and, if we're honest, they don't always meet ours. Unmet expectations are a reality of life, and I would even venture to say, a grace from God.

Because if all our expectations were met all the time, we wouldn't recognize our need for the One who will one day make all things right.

While the above statement is true, that God never changes or disappoints, the reality is that we often think he does. Most of us have at least had the fleeting sensation of disappointment towards God. Perhaps he didn't answer a specific prayer, or he answered it differently than we were expecting or in a different time frame than we desired. The longer I walk with the Lord, the more aware I have become of his sovereignty, and thus these fleeting thoughts of disappointment have become fewer and farther between. But in the early years, when God didn't meet my expectations, I faced him with arrogance, as if I knew better. Now, by the work of the Holy Spirit, when I have these feelings, I quickly recognize I'm acting like a spoiled child. It's not so much that I'm disappointed in God, just annoyed that his way is better than mine.

Do you ever feel disappointed with God or feel he hasn't met your expectations? Think about your counselees. Have you ever had a time when your expectations weren't met because the Lord didn't bring about change? How did you respond to this in your heart and in your thinking?

Join me in revisiting Moses and the Israelites. Keep in mind, the Israelites had been enslaved by the Egyptians for generations and we're picking up the story where the Lord has finally freed them. In Exodus 14, we find the Israelites on the move, led by Moses.

> *When the king of Egypt was told that the people had fled, the mind of Pharaoh and his servants was changed toward the people, and they said, "What is this we have done, that we have let Israel go from serving us?" So he made ready his chariot and took his army with him, and took six hundred chosen chariots and all the*

*other chariots of Egypt with officers over all of them. And the
Lord hardened the heart of Pharaoh king of Egypt, and he
pursued the people of Israel while the people of Israel were going
out defiantly. The Egyptians pursued them, all Pharaoh's horses
and chariots and his horsemen and his army, and overtook them
encamped at the sea, by Pi-hahiroth, in front of Baal-zephon.
(Exodus 14:5-9)*

I picture myself being an Israelite in this situation and I can't help but
think that in my self- centeredness, I would have expected God to *soften*
Pharaoh's heart, not harden it. After all, had God softened Pharaoh's
heart the escape from enslavement would have been much easier and
less frightening.

*When Pharaoh drew near, the people of Israel lifted up their eyes,
and behold, the Egyptians were marching after them, and they
feared greatly. And the people of Israel cried out to the Lord. They
said to Moses, "Is it because there are no graves in Egypt that you
have taken us away to die in the wilderness? What have you done
to us in bringing us out of Egypt? Is not this what we said to you
in Egypt: 'Leave us alone that we may serve the Egyptians'? For
it would have been better for us to serve the Egyptians than to die
in the wilderness." And Moses said to the people, "Fear not,
stand firm, and see the salvation of the Lord, which he will work
for you today. For the Egyptians whom you see today, you shall
never see again. The Lord will fight for you, and you have only to
be silent." (Exodus 14:10-14)*

Take note of the Israelites' grumblings. They would rather have stayed
slaves to the Egyptians than to be freed and die in the wilderness. Isn't
this just the kind of attitude you would expect from a sinful human?
Doesn't this seem ungrateful? Yet we see the Lord, in his faithfulness,

fighting for his people just as Moses said he would. Let's pick up this account where Moses and the Israelites are standing before the Red Sea. The Lord is speaking:

> *Lift up your staff, and stretch out your hand over the sea and divide it, that the people of Israel may go through the sea on dry ground. And I will harden the hearts of the Egyptians so that they shall go in after them, and I will get glory over Pharaoh and all his host, his chariots, and his horsemen. And the Egyptians shall know that I am the Lord, when I have gotten glory over Pharaoh, his chariots, and his horsemen.*
>
> *Then the angel of God who was going before the host of Israel moved and went behind them, and the pillar of cloud moved from before them and stood behind them, coming between the host of Egypt and the host of Israel. And there was the cloud and the darkness. And it lit up the night without one coming near the other all night.*
>
> *And as the Egyptians fled into it, the Lord threw the Egyptians into the midst of the sea. The waters returned and covered the chariots and the horsemen; of all the host of Pharaoh that had followed them into the sea, not one of them remained. But the people of Israel walked on dry ground through the sea, the waters being a wall to them on their right hand and on their left.*
>
> *Thus the Lord saved Israel that day from the hand of the Egyptians, and Israel saw the Egyptians dead on the seashore. Israel saw the great power that the Lord used against the Egyptians, so the people feared the Lord, and they believed in the Lord and in his servant Moses. (Exodus 14:16-31)*

What comes next in this account never surprises me. They worshiped God! Moses led the people in a song recounting God's goodness and how he is their strength, their song and their salvation. Then Miriam, Aaron's sister, sang to the women about God's glorious triumph while the other women praised God with tambourines! They understood, in this moment, who God was and what he had done for them. Their expectations had not only been met, but likely exceeded. I mean, who would have expected the Red Sea to be parted to create a safe passage? But, oh how we want our expectations to continue being met.

> *Then Moses made Israel set out from the Red Sea, and they went into the wilderness of Shur. They went three days in the wilderness and found no water. When they came to Marah, they could not drink the water of Marah because it was bitter; therefore it was named Marah. And the people grumbled against Moses, saying, "What shall we drink?" (Exodus 15:22-24)*

Three days! It only took three days for them to start grumbling again. And what did God do? He provided.

> *Then they came to Elim, where there were twelve springs of water and seventy palm trees, and they encamped there by the water. (Exodus 15:27)*

Was this enough to stop their grumbling?

> *They set out from Elim, and all the congregation of the people of Israel came to the wilderness of Sin, which is between Elim and Sinai, on the fifteenth day of the second month after they had departed from the land of Egypt. And the whole congregation of the people of Israel grumbled against Moses and Aaron in the wilderness, and the people of Israel said to them, "Would that we had died by the hand of the Lord in the land of Egypt, when we sat by the meat pots and ate bread to the full, for you have brought*

us out into this wilderness to kill this whole assembly with
hunger." (Exodus 16:1-3)

I don't know about you, but I like to think that after God parted the
Red Sea and sent an angel to stand guard before me and behind me
with a cloud that would separate me from the enemy, I would just trust
that he would provide food and water. I wouldn't dare grumble! Yeah,
that's what I like to think. The truth is, I probably would have been
grumbling that my feet hurt while walking through the parted waters
and I probably would have found a way to complain about the size or
shape of the cloud. I'm no different than the Israelites. When my
expectations aren't met, I grumble. And when I grumble over unmet
expectations, one word comes to mind. Idolatry.

Idolatry is anything or anyone that captures our hearts, minds and
affections more than God. Do you see that in the Israelites? Rather
than their hearts being captured by God and what he had done for
them, they were focused on their own comfort. Their dry mouths. The
rumbling in their bellies. When I get frustrated with my broken body, I
am focusing on my earthly desires. I'm idolizing the ability to run a
marathon or to simply ride a bicycle. I idolize serving. I want to be able
to take on more counselees and to serve in multiple capacities without
having to worry about my energy levels. I want more than what the
Lord is allowing me to do, and in my sinfulness, I tend to ignore the
fact that my health could be significantly worse and the fact that the
Lord has been immeasurably gracious to me.

Now, here's the rub. Doesn't it sound logical for the Israelites to have
been worried about the Egyptian army pursuing them? Isn't it right that
they'd be worried about thirsting and starving to death? Isn't my desire
to serve more a good thing? Isn't it good for a counselee to want your

undivided attention so as to move past their problems as quickly as possible?

Not necessarily.

The Israelites needed rescuing, that much we know is true. They were enslaved and needed to be freed. It would have been very easy for them to praise Moses had everything gone smoothly. Had Pharaoh's heart not been hardened and had he not pursued them with his army, God wouldn't have needed to part the Red Sea to give them safe passage. Had they immediately found water, they likely would have taken it for granted and not gathered to sing praises to God. Had food been readily available, God would not have needed to fill their camp with quail in the evening and cover the ground with manna in the morning. So why did God do these things? Why does he do anything? For his glory. For our good. And so that we will know *he* is our God.

Something I've come to recognize over the years is that God proves himself to me the most when I'm in need. Something else I've come to recognize is that I forget the very next day that he has proven himself. And then what do I do? I grumble. I look to my idols instead of my God.

Brad Bigney, in his book *Gospel Treason*, says this about idolatry:

> *At the heart of idolatry is a lack of trusting God. Here's the bottom line: Are you going to worship God, follow God, and trust God? Or are you going to cling to your idols and build your own world around them? We go other places besides God, cling to other things and people and circumstances for our security. It isn't just unbelievers who don't trust God - often, believers don't really trust him either.*

So easily and so quickly our trust drifts. It has to be continually renewed and put back in the right spot. Trust drifts. And it never drifts toward God; it's always away from him and toward our idols. And your failure to trust God doesn't just affect your relationship with God; it affects how you respond to your wife and kids, how you respond to that health problem and how you respond to that financial setback.[8]

Do you see a connection between idolatry and not trusting God? I think had the Israelites been trusting God to fulfill their needs, they wouldn't have been grumbling and idolizing their own comfort. When I'm focused on God's goodness and the fact that his grace is sufficient, I can view my health issues as an opportunity to lean on the Lord, rather than whine about my limitations and idolize those with strong, healthy bodies. When our counselees see that their problems are part of their sanctification, they can trust God in the process and let change happen in his timing, rather than rushing to "get fixed" so the suffering will end. They can then let go of idolizing their own comfort, or their time, or their . . . the list of idols is endless!

God has nothing to prove to anyone, yet he proves himself to us everyday. We speak of his goodness, we praise him for who he is, and then as soon as our expectations aren't met, what do we do? We grumble. Or something of the like. Why do we do this? I think this is when our pride comes into play. We feel justified in our desires. We think we know best. And sometimes we don't even recognize our idols, as they are often cloaked in good, respectable, reasonable things like serving and not wanting to die of thirst.

---

[8] Brad Bigney, *Gospel Treason: Betraying the Gospel with Hidden Idols* (Phillipsburg, New Jersey: P & R Publishing Company, 2012), 131.

Think about how different your life, and the lives of your counselees, would look if you relied solely on God and never allowed your trust in him to waver. When I apply this to Carol, the woman who wanted a counselor whose personal needs would never take precedence over her own, I can't help but wonder if I should have taken her on as a step of faith. I'll never know, because she's moved on. But what if I hadn't been afraid of not meeting her expectations? Perhaps the Lord led her to me because she needed her expectations to not be met. Maybe I was the perfect counselor for her because when my flare-ups forced me to stay in bed, she would be forced to rely on God that week in a different way. I shudder to think that I missed an opportunity and failed to trust in God to provide for Carol in my counseling room. But, praise God that his work was not stifled because I passed her on. God was not surprised that I didn't take her on as a counselee. God was not wringing his hands in worry wondering how he was going to help Carol now. No, God led Carol to someone else that would help her, and he is using that experience even now to teach me a lesson. For that I am grateful. I agree with Jerry Bridges in his book *Trusting God*, who says, *"God's plan is sovereign. It includes our foolish decisions as well as our wise ones."*[9]

This brings to mind a song I grew up singing, a hymn that comes to mind often. I hope it sticks with me all my days.

> *'Tis so sweet to trust in Jesus, Just to take Him at His Word;*
> *Just to rest upon His promise; Just to know, "Thus saith the Lord!"*

> *Jesus, Jesus, how I trust Him! How I've proved Him o'er and o'er; Jesus,*
> *Jesus, precious Jesus! O for grace to trust Him more!*[10]

---

[9] Jerry Bridges, *Trusting God: Even When Life Hurts* (Colorado Springs, Colorado: NAVPRESS, 1988), 170.

[10] Louisa M. R. Stead, "'Tis So Sweet to Trust in Jesus," 1882.

What's in Your Toolbox?

Whether we're fighting our own unmet expectations or we're the source of an unmet expectation, we can look to God's Word for how to respond. Through the power of the Holy Spirit, we can let go of our unmet expectations and see them as God's perfect will trumping our earthly desires. We can trust that this is for our good and his glory, and so that we may know HE is our God.

1. John 8:31-32

"So Jesus said to the Jews who had believed him, 'If you abide in my word, you are truly my disciples, and you will know the truth, and the truth will set you free.'"

What is the best way to remind yourself that God is faithful and trustworthy? Know him. If you don't know God and his character, you can't remind yourself that he is good. That he is perfect. That he is just. That he is merciful. That he is not only worthy of your trust, but of your praise. If you are in the Word daily and you make a habit of tucking his truths away in your heart, then your heart will be free to trust him. Trusting him will allow you to put to death the idols that distract and keep you grumbling.

2. Joshua 24:15

". . . choose this day whom you will serve, whether the gods your fathers served in the region beyond the River, or the gods of the Amorites in whose land you dwell. But as for me and my house, we will serve the Lord."

It's easy to tell yourself that you serve the Lord while also blindly serving your idols. Look at the areas of your life where you grumble. Trace your grumbling to the unmet expectation. Ask the Lord to show you any idols that might be hiding there. Act on what he reveals to you, and choose whom you will serve.

3. Romans 8:28

"And we know that for those who love God all things work together for good, for those who are called according to his purpose."

While your life on earth might be filled with disappointments and unmet expectations, you can rest assured that, as a child of God, your future is secure. What awaits you in paradise is beyond your wildest dreams. You can face earthly challenges and disappointments without grumbling, and with the knowledge that it is all pointing you in a heavenward direction.

4. Romans 1:21

"For although they knew God, they did not honor him as God or give thanks to him, but they became futile in their thinking, and their foolish hearts were darkened."

I love what Jerry Bridges has to say about this verse.

> *Thanksgiving is an admission of dependence. Through it we recognize that in the physical realm God "gives [us] life and breath and everything else" (Acts 17:25), and that in the spiritual realm, it is God who made us alive in Christ Jesus when*

we were dead in our transgressions and sins. Everything we are and have we owe to his bountiful grace.[11]

We honor God by trusting him.

5.   1 Thessalonians 5:18

"Give thanks in all circumstances; for this is the will of God in Christ Jesus for you."

When we grumble over unmet expectations it's because our will didn't line up with God's will. When you find yourself grumbling, stop and remind yourself that not only is God's will perfect - and yours is not - but our response should never be grumbling. Our response, in all circumstances, should be one of thanksgiving.

6.   Psalm 32:10

"Many are the sorrows of the wicked, but steadfast love surrounds the one who trusts in the Lord."

We all know the difference in how we feel, physically and mentally, when we grumble in disappointment rather than accept our circumstances with thanksgiving. When we fully trust in the Lord and surrender to his will, we are surrounded by his steadfast love. The goal is to be so trusting in God's involvement in your life that any unmet expectation can be viewed as an opportunity rather than a disappointment. That's because we know that God, in his great love for us, wants us to continue growing and being sanctified. As Jerry Bridges

---

[11] Bridges, *Trusting God*, 206.

says, *"We must see our circumstances through God's love instead of, as we are prone to do, see God's love through our circumstances."*[12]

7.   2 Corinthians 5:8-10

"Yes, we are of good courage, and we would rather be away from the body and at home with the Lord. So whether we are at home or away, we make it our aim to please him. For we must all appear before the judgment seat of Christ, so that each one may receive what is due for what he has done in the body, whether good or evil."

Since we live a life full of unmet expectations, we should remember that our aim is to please the Lord. We often grumble, giving it no thought at all, because it seems so natural to voice our disappointment. Yet, as children of God, we should encourage ourselves, as we encourage our counselees, to rest in the love of Christ, give thanks in all circumstances, and aim to please him - even through our responses to unmet expectations.

---

[12] Bridges, *Trusting God,* 149.

Encouragement

As you think about the unmet expectations in your own life, strive to unearth any idols that might be causing you to grumble. Take any fear you have of not meeting the expectations of your counselees and lay them at Jesus' feet. He cares for you. He cares for your counselee. He will provide for you both in his perfect timing.

If this chapter has revealed that trusting God is an issue with you, confess that to him. Jerry Bridges says, *"Trust is not a passive state of mind. It is a vigorous act of the soul by which we choose to lay hold on the promises of God and cling to them despite the adversity that at times seeks to overwhelm us."*[13] Just as you may need a daily reminder that God has proven himself faithful, you may also need a daily reminder that he is worthy of your trust. In fact, he is the only One in your life who is completely worthy of your trust.

- **We can trust HIM!**

Proverbs 19:21 says, "Many are the plans in the mind of a man, but it is the purpose of the Lord that will stand."

We make plans everyday, and build expectations around those plans. When our plans are foiled and our expectations aren't met, rather than being discouraged, annoyed, or rather than grumbling, let's think about the truth of Proverbs 19:21. When we trust God and when we lean joyfully into his sovereignty, we can know it is his plan that stands. It is his purpose that is fulfilled. When our focus is on God and his glory, we

---

[13] Bridges, *Trusting God*, 200.

can be flexible with the outcome of every situation rather than feeling disappointed.

- **His grace really is enough.**

2 Corinthians 12:9 states, "But he said to me, 'My grace is sufficient for you, for my power is made perfect in weakness.' Therefore I will boast all the more gladly of my weaknesses, so that the power of Christ may rest upon me."

While I still have days where I'm overcome with the limitations of my earthly body, I'm so thankful that God has used the past twenty plus years to bring me to a place where I can honestly say, I wouldn't trade this earthly body for a healthy one. My weakness has given others the opportunity to see the power of God work through me. I pray that whatever unmet expectation you are facing in your life will lead you to the same realization that God's grace is sufficient and his power is made perfect in weakness.

- **God can use our unmet expectations to help others.**

2 Corinthians 1:3-4 promises, "Blessed be the God and Father of our Lord Jesus Christ, the Father of mercies and God of all comfort, who comforts us in all our affliction, so that we may be able to comfort those who are in any affliction, with the comfort with which we ourselves are comforted by God."

I like to think that at some point the Israaelites were able to tell of their unmet expectations, admit to their grumblings, and then praise God for his provision despite their continual unfaithfulness. I pray that each of us, including our counselees, can do the same.

Personal Reflection

1. Write down a time when you did not meet your counselee's expectations. How did you deal with their emotional response?

2. List some unmet expectations in your own life and how you've responded to them.

3. What idols do you think your responses reveal?

4. What do you think your idols say about your trust in God?

5. How do you think your life would look different if you learned to handle the disappointment of unmet expectations in a more mature manner?

6. Start taking note of areas in your life where you are prone to grumble. Ask for accountability as you start making changes in your responses to unmet expectations. Ask a trusted friend or perhaps your spouse to help you recognize moments when you are responding poorly to unmet expectations.

Chapter 5

When the Counselor needs Counseling

When God gives gifts to his church, He wraps them up in people.

Bill Lane

Lisa lost her son to a drug overdose and came to me for help processing through her grief. Although her son had died several years prior to our meeting, Lisa was still living in a state of shock. She was overcome with sadness, confusion, anger and resentment and then to make matters worse, she had turned to alcohol to escape reality. As I quickly learned, her son's death was an added layer to a life already piled high with trauma.

I don't mind confessing that I lost control of the counseling room on day one. Lisa entered the room in mid-sentence, already crying, and ready to pour out her wrath. Our time together, for weeks, consisted of her crying to the point of shaking, causing her words to become muddled and disjointed. When she spoke of the murder trial for the man who gave her son the lethal drugs, she would point her finger at me, as if I were that man, and yell all the degrading and incriminating words she would like to yell at him.

Lisa spoke so quickly and with such animation that it was difficult for me to break in. She would raise her voice and become even more agitated if I tried to offer her comfort. Her bitterness was equally directed at God. She only offered arguments against his Word, finding no comfort there. It became clear to me, from the beginning, that Lisa just wanted someone to listen, someone to take it. And because the man she wanted to lash out at was behind bars and inaccessible, she lashed out at me.

I found myself having anxiety, especially the night before our sessions. In between sessions she would often text me in the middle of the night, and I would wake up with dread over what awaited me in those messages. Week after week, Lisa would leave the session and I would sit down and cry; really I would weep. I felt extremely inadequate, yet extraordinarily qualified. Let me explain.

My husband and I lost our daughter, Grace Ann, going into our second trimester. Grace was developed enough that we were able to hold her in our hand and marvel over the outline of her toes and fingers. We could see the slits of her eyes and her perfect little nose. She was precious. What I didn't talk much about at the time was what it did to me psychologically. For weeks after her burial I had nightmares of her coming up out of the ground. She would be covered in dirt and ask us why we kept her outside. This made for many restless nights, but the days weren't much better. I often thought I heard a baby crying in the next room and I would often turn and see a little girl peeking at me from around the corner. I thought I was losing my mind.

About five years later I lost my dad. He had been living with Parkinson's disease and dementia and, in a moment of confusion, took his own life. As you can imagine, this left us in shock, with questions, and guilt of not seeing the signs of his condition more clearly. This sent me back into a depression that I had only ever felt once before, when we lost our daughter.

A few years later my only sibling was murdered. Our family was thrust into an ongoing investigation that left us not only exhausted, but confused and infuriated. We were faced with the reality that our questions might never be answered, and that there might never be justice this side of heaven. A murderer was walking free, living life as normal, while we were left to pick up the broken pieces that death leaves behind.

When I first heard Lisa's story I felt very inadequate, as I do in almost every first session. Yet, as you can see, I've had experience with grief. And more specifically to her situation, I have experience with wrongful death and police investigations. The darkness that comes from that kind of suffering is all too familiar. However, I've always known that if I was faithful to share my history of loss, counseling was a way God would redeem that pain. My own experience of walking through the veil of tears gives me an insight and a compassion for my suffering counselees that I wouldn't have otherwise. With that in mind, I looked at my past sufferings as a blessing, as part of my sanctification, and also as a means to help others.

Almost a decade after my brother was killed I claimed to have adequately dealt with my grief. I had put each of those losses in their own little box and tucked them away on a corner shelf in my heart. I was fully functional. I felt joy in the Lord, and while I thought of our daughter, my dad and my brother almost daily, I would have told you my grief had turned from sorrow to sweet memories. My grief hadn't gone away, but it had changed. I was fine.

Enter Lisa. Her aggression took me back to an abusive boyfriend, which triggered a fear response. It was something else from my past I thought I had put to rest. As she pointed her finger and yelled at me, I found myself paralyzed; I felt trapped. She was so unstable that, as she sat before me weeping, I feared speaking. Trying to comfort her was like trying to pet a porcupine in defense mode. As her body shook from grief, mine trembled in fear. As she choked on her words about how much she missed her son, I felt the heaviness of my own loss. As she asked her questions, expecting me to have answers, I was reminded of my own unanswered questions. When Lisa described the crime scene of her son's death, my mind started forming images of what my brother's crime scene might have looked like. I found myself reliving moments that I had no desire to relive.

I cried more during those weeks than I did during my three seasons of grief combined. I was gutted. Lisa's despair seemed to be contagious and while I knew I needed to live out 2 Corinthians 1:4 and comfort her with the comfort I, myself, had received from God, I suddenly couldn't recall the comfort I had received. I found myself stepping back almost two decades and actively grieving all over again. I felt like a dark cloud had settled over us both, and it scared me.

This is when I realized that sometimes the counselor needs counseling, so I reached out to a fellow biblical counselor. My husband was already aware of the situation because my emotional distress was obvious. These two people became a support system that would not only benefit me but Lisa as well. I was able to glean wisdom from my support system not only to deal with my own grief, but to bring order back to the counseling room, and finally take steps to help Lisa. I needed help seeing past my own emotions so that I could speak directly to Lisa about hers. She had every right to grieve, and she was welcome to cry through the entire session if she wanted. She was not, however, welcome to yell at me as though I were the criminal. She needed to treat me with respect, and I needed the courage to tell her this. Yet, standing up to Lisa seemed as impossible as standing up to that abusive boyfriend.

I needed help with this case. I needed guidance, wisdom and encouragement. While I spent time telling Lisa that she wasn't alone, I needed to know that I wasn't alone, and my support system reminded me of that. At the head of this chapter is a quote from Bill Lane, a pastor I knew many years ago in Tennessee. He was known for saying, "When God gives gifts to his church, he wraps them up in people." I have this hanging in my office and I think of it often. God, in his wisdom, created us to be relational. And this makes sense - the Trinity means that God is, in his essence, relational. I love the saying that he gives gifts to his church wrapped up in people; I think that's true of everyone in my life. They're all gifts that he has given me. But the church itself is a gift to the church. We are a unit. We are co-heirs. We are eternally connected. We are, in every sense of the phrase, forever family.

When God said in Genesis 2:18 that it is not good for man to be alone, he wasn't just making a statement about Adam. He was making a statement about his design for humanity as a whole. If God intended us to live out our lives on our own, the creation mandate wouldn't exist. Whether you are being fruitful and multiplying by making babies or by making disciples, clearly we are to be relational. We wouldn't need Romans 12:15 to tell us to rejoice with those who rejoice and mourn with those who mourn if we were intended to rejoice and mourn alone. My point is, your counselee understands they can't do it alone, so we as counselors should understand that too. There are times when the counselor needs counseling.

Think back on the account of Moses and the Israelites. Does my experience with Lisa bring anything in particular to mind? Let's read Exodus 18 together.

Jethro, the priest of Midian, Moses' father-in-law, heard of all that God had done for Moses and for Israel his people, how the Lord had brought Israel out of Egypt. Now Jethro, Moses' father-in-law, had taken Zipporah, Moses' wife, after he had sent her home, along with her two sons. The name of the one was Gershom (for he said, "I have been a sojourner in a foreign land"), and the name of the other, Eliezer (for he said, "The God of my father was my help, and delivered me from the sword of Pharaoh"). Jethro, Moses' father-in-law, came with his sons and his wife to Moses in the wilderness where he was encamped at the mountain of God. And when he sent word to Moses, "I, your father-in-law Jethro, am coming to you with your wife and her two sons with her," Moses went out to meet his father-in-law and bowed down and kissed him. And they asked each other of their welfare and went into the tent. Then Moses told his father-in-law all that the Lord had done to Pharaoh and to the Egyptians for Israel's sake, all the hardship that had come upon them in the way, and how the Lord had delivered them. And Jethro rejoiced for all the good that the Lord had done to Israel, in that he had delivered them out of the hand of the Egyptians.

Jethro said, "Blessed be the Lord, who has delivered you out of the hand of the Egyptians and out of the hand of Pharaoh and has delivered the people from under the hand of the Egyptians. Now I know that the Lord is greater than all gods, because in this affair they dealt arrogantly with the people." And Jethro, Moses' father-in-law, brought a burnt offering and sacrifices to God; and

*Aaron came with all the elders of Israel to eat bread with Moses'
father-in-law before God.*

*The next day Moses sat to judge the people, and the people stood
around Moses from morning till evening. When Moses'
father-in-law saw all that he was doing for the people, he said,
"What is this that you are doing for the people? Why do you sit
alone, and all the people stand around you from morning till
evening?" And Moses said to his father-in-law, "Because the
people come to me to inquire of God; when they have a dispute,
they come to me and I decide between one person and another, and
I make them know the statutes of God and his laws." Moses'
father-in-law said to him, "What you are doing is not good. You
and the people with you will certainly wear yourselves out, for the
thing is too heavy for you. You are not able to do it alone. Now
obey my voice; I will give you advice, and God be with you! You
shall represent the people before God and bring their cases to God,
and you shall warn them about the statutes and the laws, and
make them know the way in which they must walk and what they
must do. Moreover, look for able men from all the people, men
who fear God, who are trustworthy and hate a bribe, and place
such men over the people as chiefs of thousands, of hundreds, of
fifties, and of tens. And let them judge the people at all times.
Every great matter they shall bring to you, but any small matter
they shall decide themselves. So it will be easier for you, and they
will bear the burden with you. If you do this, God will direct you,
you will be able to endure, and all this people also will go to their
place in peace."*

*So Moses listened to the voice of his father-in-law and did all that
he had said. Moses chose able men out of all Israel and made
them heads over the people, chiefs of thousands, of hundreds, of
fifties, and of tens. And they judged the people at all times. Any*

His Power, Our Weakness

hard case they brought to Moses, but any small matter they
decided themselves. Then Moses let his father-in-law depart, and
he went away to his own country.

I've always wondered if Moses appeared overwhelmed or if Jethro just had the wisdom to see the potential of Moses wearing himself out. Either way, Jethro's advice was golden. Moses needed help. He simply couldn't continue carrying the burden of the people alone. And if you noticed, Jethro isn't just concerned about Moses, he's also concerned about the people. Moses is essentially counseling *thousands* of people; they're coming to him with their issues and disagreements and he sorts it out. Imagine the emotional toll that would take on anyone. I've never had more than six counselees at any one time and I thought *that* was overwhelming! What Jethro helps Moses see is that he doesn't have to carry this burden alone. And neither do we.

Imagine what would have happened had I not reached out for help during my time with Lisa.

First, I likely would have continued spiraling down into depression. I would have given into fear and let Lisa continue to dominate the relationship. We would have sat for hours with her venting and me soaking it in, contaminating my heart and mind.

Second, Lisa would never have been held accountable for her sinful behavior. I would have continued to allow her to yell at me and take advantage of our time together. Without encouragement and accountability I might never have spoken up, made changes, and tried harder to point Lisa to God's Word.

90

Third, my support system would have missed out on the blessing of bearing my burden. They would have missed out on seeing me respond to the wisdom the Lord imparted to them. They wouldn't have seen the Spirit working in me, giving me the strength to make changes. And they would have missed an opportunity to praise God for his faithfulness.

Biblical counseling is a burden of love and we don't have to carry that burden alone.

What's in your Toolbox?

Our counselees aren't the only ones who believe lies. We do too. The enemy wants trauma from our past to resurface and distract us from helping others. He wants us to feel paralyzed and weak. He wants us to believe that people will question our ability to counsel if we ask for counseling ourselves. But friends, these are lies from the pit of hell. We must fight against the enemy and know that we serve a God who was there with us when we first experienced our trauma and he is with us each and every time it comes back to haunt us. He has not left us to suffer alone. He is with us, and he has given us brothers and sisters to help carry us through.

1.   Hebrews 10:24-25

"And let us consider how to stir up one another to love and good works, not neglecting to meet together, as is the habit of some, but encouraging one another, and all the more as you see the Day drawing near."

God isn't the head of a million one-person churches. He is the head of *the* church that is made up of *all* his children, which means we have brothers and sisters who can walk us down the dark roads. If you find yourself with a hard case that has stirred up past trauma, know you can ask for help. Asking for help is not a sign of weakness, it's a sign of wisdom.

2. 2 Corinthians 12:9

"But he said to me, 'My grace is sufficient for you, for my power is made perfect in weakness.' Therefore I will boast all the more gladly of my weaknesses, so that the power of Christ may rest upon me. For the sake of Christ, then, I am content with weaknesses, insults, hardships, persecutions, and calamities. For when I am weak, then I am strong."

We all have experiences, circumstances, situations and wounds that are difficult for us to bear. Perhaps this describes your past or your present. It is in these times that we can look to God and know, with confidence, that his grace is sufficient. His power is made perfect in our weakness. When we lean into him in our times of weakness, we glorify him by trusting him and by acknowledging that he is our refuge. We glorify Jesus when we draw on his strength to endure and rejoice in our suffering.

3. Romans 8:3-5

"Not only that, but we rejoice in our sufferings, knowing that suffering produces endurance, and endurance produces character, and character produces hope, and hope does not put us to shame, because God's love has been poured into our hearts through the Holy Spirit who has been given to us."

We've all had counselees come to us who just want their suffering to end. They want us to pull out the easy button and push it with speed and gusto. If we're honest, we've been there too. No one likes to suffer. But by God's grace, our suffering is never in vain. One way that he uses our suffering for our good is to use it for our sanctification. I can clearly see how I have grown in endurance, character, and hope through my sufferings. When we allow ourselves to sit in our sufferings, rather than trying to dull the pain, we are sanctified and God is glorified.

4. Isaiah 49:13

"Sing for joy, O heavens, and exult, O earth; break forth, O mountains, into singing! For the Lord has comforted his people and will have compassion on his afflicted."

The Lord shows us comfort and compassion in so many ways, often in ways we don't even recognize. One way he does this is by gifting us with brothers and sisters that will point us to Jesus when we lose sight of the cross. We are never alone in our suffering, even when we feel that we are. We can turn our mourning into song and praise him for how he lavishes his love on us.

5. Romans 15:13

"May the God of hope fill you with all joy and peace in believing, so that by the power of the Holy Spirit you may abound in hope."

We tell our counselees that, even in their darkest moments, there is joy to be found in the Lord. Through the work of the Holy Spirit, we can have peace even in the most chaotic circumstances. And because of these things, by the power of the Holy Spirit we can have hope. We can rest in our salvation and have an expectant hope of what's to come. The good news is, this isn't just true for our counselees, this is true for the counselor also.

6. Hebrews 13:6

"So we can confidently say, 'The Lord is my helper; I will not fear; what can man do to me?'"

Your counselee's trauma may remind you of your own. Your counselee might remind you of an abuser from your past. Your grief might resurface as you walk your counselee through their own. But with the Lord as your helper, you need not be afraid. You can face whatever is to come with confidence because the Lord is your helper.

7. Psalm 40:17

"As for me, I am poor and needy, but the Lord takes thought for me. You are my help and my deliverer; do not delay, O my God!"

Whatever you're facing, inside or outside the counseling room, the Lord takes thought of you. You are never out of his reach, his thoughts or his care. He is your help and your deliverer. It is to your benefit and his glory to admit when you are poor and needy. Just as Jesus lives to intercede for us, God delights in helping his children. You need not suffer alone.

Encouragement

- ## **Emotions in the counseling room are a good thing**

Romans 12:15 says, *"Rejoice with those who rejoice, weep with those who weep."*

Situations may arise, like mine with Lisa, where order should be restored to the counseling room. But we shouldn't be afraid of our counselees showing emotion even if it triggers our own. This is one way to demonstrate our love and genuine interest for the counselee. If your counselee tells you that in between sessions their marriage was restored, you should rejoice with them! You wouldn't sit there emotionless. In the same way, when your counselee feels safe enough with you to let the tears flow, it's more than appropriate for yours to flow too.

- ## **We serve a God who sees**

Genesis 16:13 says, *"So she called the name of the Lord who spoke to her, 'You are a God of seeing,' for she said, 'Truly here I have seen him who looks after me.'"*

I have had so many Hagar moments in my life - times when I felt alone and forgotten. But then God works in my life in a way that I know, without a shadow of a doubt, that he sees me. There is so much comfort and encouragement to be found in Hagar's story. We serve a God who sees our joy and our pain. He sees us and he looks after us.

- **God will redeem your suffering**

Romans 8:28 promises, *"And we know that for those who love God all things work together for good, for those who are called according to his purpose."*

For children of God, I believe there are two elements at work here. First, I do believe that God redeems our suffering here on earth. Sometimes we see it played out, sometimes we don't. As biblical counselors, I think any suffering we've experienced helps us in the counseling room and is a form of redemption. Second, I believe this verse also speaks to our eternal life. Our sufferings on earth are molding us in our sanctification and are pointing us to our heavenly home where there will be no more suffering. This is good news for us and for our counselees who know the Lord.

Personal Reflections

1. Why do you think it is just as important for us, as it is for our counselees, to know we serve a God who sees?

2. What do you think about the statement, "Asking for help is a sign of wisdom, not weakness"?

3. How would you help a fellow counselor who started reliving her trauma during a counseling session?

4. What scriptures bring you comfort when your past trauma comes to the surface?

5. How do you think you would deal with an aggressive counselee like Lisa?

6. Imagine your own past trauma has clouded your judgment towards a particular counselee. How might you handle this?

Chapter 6

The Importance of Personal Soul Care

The heart cannot love what the mind does not know.

Jen Wilkin, *Women of the Word*

About fifteen years ago I started a ministry for women struggling with sexual sin. This has allowed me to walk with women who are sex addicts, some who have no desire for sex at all and those who fall at varying degrees in the middle of these two extremes. What I found early on with this ministry was that the vast majority of these women had experienced some sort of sexual trauma or abuse. These women could pinpoint exactly what triggered their addiction or lack of interest, which often allowed me to help them process their pasts.

Knowing this, it shouldn't surprise you that the majority of the books I read, the training I sought and the biblical references I memorized were focused on these issues. My husband and I have spoken at marriage retreats about sexual sin and how to affair proof your marriage. We have counseled couples who were struggling in this area and we currently cover the sex and intimacy portion of the premarital counseling in our church family. We have a reputation for wanting to help build strong marriages and healthy marriage beds and because of this, I have become affectionately known as the "sex lady" in our church body - which has made for some awkward Sunday morning conversations in line at the bathroom. When I let it be known that I was pursuing certification as a biblical counselor, women started coming to me for issues unrelated to the bedroom. While sex-related issues are still my passion, it's been nice to cover more topics and speak to a wider variety of issues.

However, speaking to a wider variety of issues means I need to know something about those issues. For all those years, if someone came to me about a sexual issue, I could open my Bible and immediately dig in. But that wasn't the case the first time I had a counselee with an eating disorder or an alcohol addiction. I had to reorient myself with God's Word and find applications that went beyond the bedroom. I enjoyed this challenge, but it was a challenge. During my certification process the Lord seemed to bring me a variety of cases all at once and I not only had to devote study time in God's Word, but I also had to familiarize myself with other available resources.

Picture this. I was digging into God's Word, trying to find applications and narratives that spoke to the issues my counselees were facing. My supervisor would recommend books for my counselees but I didn't feel good about assigning them without having read them myself. So, in those early days if I assigned a counselee a book, I would read it along with them. This means at any one time I was reading through three or four different books along with God's Word.

The most challenging part of becoming a certified biblical counselor was that I still had all the other obligations in my life. I still had a family to feed, a house to clean, and friends to fellowship with. We still had family game nights, church family gatherings, and small group Bible studies. I was on the teaching rotation for our ladies group and I still, at some point, wanted alone time with my husband. Of course, I needed to sleep. Factor in my health issues and chronic fatigue and I think you'll agree I could have used more hours in my day. Now, there are people with much busier schedules than mine, I know that, but my point is that life doesn't stop just because you choose to serve as a biblical counselor. Time management is crucial and I failed miserably. I hope sharing my experience will help you make better choices.

The major mistake I made was counting the hours in the day, realizing that something had to give, and allowing my personal time with the Lord to be the something that got sacrificed. Now, let me be clear - it wasn't a conscious decision. I didn't say to myself, "I'm not going to spend time with the Lord for my own personal growth and edification. That can wait till later." No, I told myself that I would grow while reading and studying for the benefit of my counselee. True enough, I did, since I was able to apply nuggets of truth to my own life from the books I was reading. The problem was that somewhere along the way I stopped applying what I was reading to myself. My focus was on my counselees and how the Bible spoke to *their* lives. Period.

After two or three months of this, I hit a wall. I'll discuss this more in the next chapter but for now I just want to focus on what I felt: burned out. I remember telling my husband that I felt distant from the Lord, which was odd because I was spending more time in the Word than usual and I was reading all these fantastic books that applied God's Word in eloquent and creative ways. Yet, the Lord seemed far away, and his Word seemed like a salve for someone else's soul.

My prayer life began to suffer as well. It started out strong. I was praying for all my counselees throughout the week and spending time in prayer before each session. I asked for wisdom, compassion and for the Holy Spirit to bring about change in the counselee's life. I thought I was doing everything "right." But as my relationship with the Lord felt more and more disconnected, so did my prayer life. I still prayed, but it became something I did out of habit, or even worse, obligation. My heart wasn't in it.

Looking back, it reminds me of a married couple who spend all their time focusing on the kids. The kids are all they talk about, even in their alone time. Providing for the kids is why they work so hard. All the books they read are about parenting. Then what happens when the kids are gone? The couple realizes they have nothing in common except the one thing that isn't there anymore. Now, all analogies fail at some point but you get the idea. I was using God to help me "parent" my counselees - his children. But I wasn't working on my "marriage" to the Lord. I wasn't investing in *my* role as the bride of Christ. I was so focused on making him known to my counselees that I neglected to know him myself.

Balance is the key. As Christ followers we should already be perpetual students. Now as biblical counselors we need to always be reading, familiarizing ourselves with new resources and we should be studying God's Word with our counselees in mind. But we cannot neglect our own relationship with the Lord. First and foremost we should be walking with him for our own personal growth. We can't be effective in our ministry if we're neglecting our own soul care.

You don't have to make the same mistake I did to find yourself in a dry spiritual season. A million and one things can distract us from our time with the Lord. I was discussing this recently with my friend and co-laborer, Renee. Here's what she had to say.

> *When I am intentionally spending personal time in the Word for devotion and the deepening of my own relationship with the Lord, I am more prepared to guide and counsel others. I can tell when*

I've really studied scripture, dissected and unpacked it. When I have, it's in my heart and it just flows out in the counseling room. When I haven't spent time in the Word for my own growth, then I struggle to know where to take my counselee in the Word during our session or I struggle with assigning homework. When I'm in the midst of it and I'm stumbling all over the place because I haven't been in the Word, I'm so disappointed and convicted. I know in my heart that my Lord is grieved that I haven't been dwelling in His Word enough. And I am not well prepared to guide my counselee. But when I'm immersed in the Word it flows out naturally.

We all have a time, a season, when life happens and we find it difficult to be in the Word on a regular basis. Hands down, it affects the counseling session. We can stumble around, try and cover it up, to hide it, but who are we hiding that from? God knows. He knows and is gracious time after time to lead us when we stumble.

The truth is, there is a fine line between studying for the counselee, so that when I'm in the room I'm able to give specific guidance, and studying for my own heart and my own relationship with the Lord and then offer that to the counselee. When I study for my own heart and my own growth, the Lord uses that in the counseling room in a very authentic and organic way.

Have you ever found yourself struggling in the counseling room because you neglected your personal time with the Lord? Renee is right. You can put on an act and try to hide this from your counselee, but you can't hide it from God. This is when you should take a moment and pray. Ask God to forgive you for neglecting your relationship with him, and then surrender your pride and ask him to lead this session.

The reality is, God leads the session whether we ask him to or not. He is the great counselor, not us. But our negligence gives us the opportunity to be humble before the Lord, and if you so choose, before your counselee as well.

While there are lessons to be learned and growth that comes about during dry seasons, nothing compares to the joy in having a healthy, active, growing relationship with our Heavenly Father. When you're in the Word for your own edification and your heart and mind are full of his truths, it pours out in the counseling room. Your joy and reliance on the Lord will be evident and will not only increase your faith, but that of your counselee as well.

Imagine your spiritual life in the context of feast or famine. In times of famine you are hungry and irritable and you have nothing to share. But in times of feast, your spiritual belly is full, your cheeks have color, your face shows not only contentment but satisfaction and you have more than enough to spare. What you have in abundance flows out in every aspect of your life, including the counseling room. I asked Renee for an example of when this has happened in her life. Here's what she had to say.

> *In my personal studies I had been in Jonah and so that was fresh in my mind. I was at the end of a counseling session and had no real direction on where to take her for homework so I asked her to read Jonah. After she left I kept thinking, "Jonah? Why Jonah?" I had no idea why I asked her to read Jonah. It made no sense but I decided just to trust it. When she came back the next week she said, "I wondered why you asked me to read Jonah but now I know. This put words to my pain and my hurt that I've never had words for. I've been in the darkness with the seaweed and couldn't get myself out of it and this gave words to my pain." And*

I knew then, that's why I assigned her Jonah. Following the lead
of the Holy Spirit will always bear fruit.

This is such a good reminder of how God is in control, inside and outside the counseling room. If we trust him to lead us through his Word during the week in our personal study time, we can trust that he will use it in the counseling room as well. When we neglect our own personal time with the Lord, we miss opportunities for him to teach us and then by extension teach our counselees. But let's be honest, most of us experience a dry season at one point or another. It's bound to happen. I asked Renee to describe what it's like for her to push through during a dry spiritual season when she feels disconnected from the Lord.

I hate it. It could be that it's a dry season, or I'm just tired of
giving what I consider "everything" and I have a cynical attitude.
Or maybe my marriage is in a dry spell and we have to go in
together to do marriage counseling. Whatever is causing me to feel
disconnected from the Lord, in those times, a full reliance on God
is what matters. You have to leave yourself outside the counseling
room and walk in obedience to the Lord. Isn't that what He
wants of us at all times?

When you're in the Word and seeing things clearly and your
marriage is going well, your spiritual well is filled up and things
seem to flow well in the counseling room. But, if you're tired,
overwhelmed, not getting along with your husband, having troubles
of your own or in your church body, it is so hard to step into the
next counseling session. For me, it is likely that I haven't relied
fully on God for my own personal struggles, and the result is a dry
season. It's on me, not God. He has been present even though I
have not. But you have to leave all that at the door and focus on

the counselee. The counsel you are about to give from the Word will likely speak just as much to your own heart to convict, rebuke, and refresh. We have to rely on God to give us what we need and to give the counselee what she needs. Without God, it is just empty counsel.

There are times I don't think I am qualified enough to be counseling women through their current life issues. The reality is, I am not. But God. God is the one who gives guidance to the women in the room. I am His mouthpiece and servant. When I can fully rely on God and take the focus off my insecurities it makes a difference.

I pray you find encouragement in knowing you're not the only one to ever experience a spiritual dry spell. We know this happens but we also know it's hard to admit. It's easy to convince ourselves that as biblical counselors we should be super spiritual, that we shouldn't have problems of our own, and that we absolutely shouldn't have spiritual lulls. So when those things happen, we're quick to ignore them. We keep trudging ahead, pushing through and doing our best to hide it from everyone around us. What we need to remember is that we are no different from our counselees. We, too, have issues that distract us and pull us away from our time with the Lord. Sometimes we're distracted by earthly pleasures like sports, scrolling on social media or curling up with a good work of fiction. But we can also be distracted by kingdom work. We can serve the kingdom to the point of neglecting our own spiritual needs. We can work tirelessly at "good things" and not take the time to refill our spiritual cup that is purposely tipped to pour out on others.

We recently voted in a new elder to serve our church family and, when our pastor was praying over him and his wife, he prayed that the church would not become a mistress. Our pastor understands that we can serve to the point of neglecting those closest to us. This can also be said of our relationship with the Lord. As biblical counselors, we need to watch out for this pitfall. We can and should serve our counselees to the point of emptying our cup, but if we don't take the time to sit with the Lord, meditate on his Word, and allow him to refill our cup, we will run on empty until the fumes stink so bad our counselees will run the other way.

In her book *Satisfy My Thirsty Soul*, Linda Dillow shares her own similar experience. She describes a scene most of us can relate to. She desired intimacy with God but as she felt the tug to sit with him and actually experience that intimacy, she found herself saying, *"Lord, I have to prepare a Bible study, I'll come later"* or, *"Lord, I have to cook a meal for some of your children, I promise I'll come later."* And then she admits,

> But *"later" never came. I was just too busy doing good things for him... It's so important to be able to say, "I am not primarily a worker for God; I am first and foremost a lover of God. This is who I am." All of us need to be lovers who work rather than workers who love. But I was a worker who loved. The result was overload and burnout.*[14]

Meditate on that for a moment. *We need to be lovers who work rather than workers who love.* Dillow goes on to say, *"When our priorities become turned around, and we place more emphasis on loving others than on loving God, we are headed for spiritual and physical exhaustion."*[15] This is exactly what happened to me. It's happened on a smaller scale multiple times over the years and if I'm not mindful, it will happen again. When you focus on loving your counselee without first focusing on loving God, you *will* get burned out.

---

[14] Linda Dillow, *Satisfy My Thirsty Soul* (Colorado Springs, Colorado: NavPress, 2007), 18.
[15] Dillow, *Satisfy My Thirsty Soul*, 19.

You will find yourself scrambling in the counseling room and realizing you weren't loving your counselee that well after all. How could you? The love you would offer would simply come from head knowledge, what you know to be true. What you want to offer our counselees is an authentic love that flows abundantly from the Holy Spirit who dwells in you as the wellspring of life.

We don't want to take our counselees to a well, pulling up the bucket to offer them a drink while relying on our own efforts. No, we want to take our counselees to the feet of Jesus, to the living water. We love our counselees best when we first love the Lord. We love our counselees best by relying on the Lord to lead us in the counseling room, not by cramming in as many resources as possible so that we know as much as we can. No, we love our counselees best by going to Jesus, sitting at his feet, and asking our counselees to join us there.

Let's look at Exodus 33: 7-23.

> *Now Moses used to take the tent and pitch it outside the camp, far off from the camp, and he called it the tent of meeting. And everyone who sought the Lord would go out to the tent of meeting, which was outside the camp. Whenever Moses went out to the tent, all the people would rise up, and each would stand at his tent door, and watch Moses until he had gone into the tent. When Moses entered the tent, the pillar of cloud would descend and stand at the entrance of the tent, and the Lord would speak with Moses. And when all the people saw the pillar of cloud standing at the entrance of the tent, all the people would rise up and worship, each at his tent door. **Thus the Lord used to speak to Moses face to face, as a man speaks to his friend**. When Moses turned again into the camp, his assistant Joshua the son of Nun, a young man, would not depart from the tent.*

Moses said to the Lord, "See, you say to me, 'Bring up this people,' but you have not let me know whom you will send with me. Yet you have said, 'I know you by name, and you have also found favor in my sight.' Now therefore, if I have found favor in your sight, **please show me now your ways, that I may know you** *in order to find favor in your sight. Consider too that this nation is your people." And he said, "My presence will go with you, and I will give you rest." And he said to him, "If your presence will not go with me, do not bring us up from here. For how shall it be known that I have found favor in your sight, I and your people? Is it not in your going with us, so that we are distinct, I and your people, from every other people on the face of the earth?"*

And the Lord said to Moses, "This very thing that you have spoken I will do, for you have found favor in my sight, and I know you by name." **Moses said, "Please show me your glory."** *And he said, "I will make all my goodness pass before you and will proclaim before you my name 'The Lord.' And I will be gracious to whom I will be gracious, and will show mercy on whom I will show mercy. But," he said, "you cannot see my face, for man shall not see me and live." And the Lord said, "Behold, there is a place by me where you shall stand on the rock, and while my glory passes by I will put you in a cleft of the rock, and I will cover you with my hand until I have passed by. Then I will take away my hand, and you shall see my back, but my face shall not be seen."* (Bold text added.)

Pay particular attention to the words in bold. The Lord used to speak to Moses face to face, as a man speaks to his friend. Is this how you approach your alone time with the Lord? Do you sit with your Bible, in prayer or in worship, hoping to know more about him or to know HIM better? Moses is a great example of how we should approach our time with God. He asked God to show him his glory so that he might know him better. Do you dig into the Word with the sole purpose of connecting dots for your counselee or with the purpose of seeing God's glory?

Friends, it's imperative that we take time for personal soul care. Taking time to sit before the Lord, to meditate on his Word, to talk to him, to listen and to worship – these are all the ways we not only care for ourselves, but for our counselees. Do you think Moses would have had the strength to carry on leading the Israelites had he not been actively striving to know God better? Here we see that God talked to Moses face to face the way that a man speaks to a friend and Moses is STILL trying to know him better! Whether you've been a Christ follower for five years or fifty years, getting to know him better should always be the goal. This should drive us to sit still before him on a daily basis.

Milton Vincent speaks about this in his book *A Gospel Primer*. Consider his words.

> *The gospel serves as the means by which God daily constructs me into what he wants me to be and also serves as the channel through which he gives me my inheritance every day of my Christian life. Hence, it could be said that the gospel contains all that I need "for life and godliness." It is for this reason that God tells me to be steadfastly entrenched in the gospel at all times and never allow myself to be moved from there. The mere fact that God tells me to stay inside the gospel at all times must mean that he intends to supply all my needs as long as I am abiding in that place of luxury.*[16]

---

[16] Milton Vincent, *A Gospel Primer for Christians: Learning to See the Glories of God's Love* (Bemidji, Minnesota: Focus Publishing, 2008), 18-19.

"Abiding in that place of luxury." I love that! I also love the idea of staying inside the gospel at all times. A practical application of this is illustrated by a current counselee of mine who is haunted by abusive language that has degraded and oppressed her for years. I ask her to speak truth to herself when her thoughts are consumed with these lies. But what do I mean by that? I mean, stay in the gospel. Preach the gospel to yourself. Allow the gospel to remind you of who you are and whose you are. But, no matter how many times I tell her to do this, if she's not IN the gospel, the life-giving truths won't be in her heart. Because she is young in her faith and is growing into her spiritual disciplines, I stressed to her the importance of being in the Word daily. She can't preach the gospel to herself if she isn't familiar with the gospel.

This is no different for us. We can't guide our counselees through the Bible if we aren't familiar with it and we can't help them get to know God if we ourselves are living like strangers to him. What we want is for our counselees to see us excited about our walk with the Lord. We want to tell of his greatness, not only because we've heard about it, but because we've seen it for ourselves. We should point to the great counselor, not because we know the Bible calls him that, but because we've seen him in action. We need to assure our counselee that God is a God of comfort, not because we've heard that in countless sermons, but because we've experienced his comfort. When our counselee is feeling hopeless, we should point her to the source of hope with confidence because we actively draw from that source.

Meditate on 2 Peter 3:13-18 for a moment.

> *But according to his promise we are waiting for new heavens and a new earth in which righteousness dwells. Therefore, beloved, since you are waiting for these, be diligent to be found by him without spot or blemish, and at peace. And count the patience of our Lord as salvation, just as our beloved brother Paul also wrote to you*

according to the wisdom given him, as he does in all his letters when he speaks in them of these matters. There are some things in them that are hard to understand, which the ignorant and unstable twist to their own destruction, as they do the other Scriptures. You therefore, beloved, knowing this beforehand, take care that you are not carried away with the error of lawless people and lose your own stability. **But grow in the grace and knowledge of our Lord and Savior Jesus Christ**. *To him be the glory both now and to the day of eternity. Amen.* (Bold text added.)

When I think about being carried away with the error of lawless people, I don't just think about those who twist the scriptures. I also think about how the world bends over backwards to distract us from what our focus should be. While *we* sing to the Lord, "Be thou my vision," the world sings to us, "Let *me* be thy vision." Our personal struggles sing, "There is no other vision" and when we feel the desire for intimacy with our heavenly Father, our flesh often sings, "That vision can wait till later."

Friends, the Lord longs for you to give him your full attention, to grow in your knowledge of him and to sit quietly and know he is God. He doesn't desire this because he's arrogant and self-centered. He longs for this because he knows what he has to offer. He longs to lavish you with his love, to woo you with his gentle spirit and keep you in a state of awe at his greatness. You may think you're missing out or being neglectful when you take time to sit with the Lord, because other things have to wait when he's your priority. But the reality is, you're missing out on more than you know when you neglect your time with him.

When you sit with him, when you abide in him, when you take the time to bask in his goodness and rest in the promises of his lavish love, the distractions of the world should melt away. It's in those moments that your cup will begin to refill. It is there that you will begin to know your heavenly Father more intimately.

What's in your Toolbox?

Have you ever been prescribed painkillers or blood pressure medication? Something you had to take on a regular schedule in order to feel better? Have you ever noticed how tempting it is to stop taking the medication once you do feel better even though the doctor's orders are to finish every last pill? This is often how we treat our time with the Lord. When things aren't going so great, we throw ourselves at his feet, dig into his Word and pray with passion. But once we start feeling better, our visits become fewer and farther between. Let us fill our toolboxes with reminders of why visits aren't enough. We need to abide in him.

1.   Philippians 4:7

"And the peace of God, which surpasses all understanding, will guard your hearts and your minds in Christ Jesus."

Spending time with the Lord doesn't guarantee your life circumstances will change. But spending time with him, learning more about him, and continuing to grow your relationship with him WILL bring about change in your heart and in your mind.

2.   Psalm 119:105

"Your word is a lamp to my feet and a light to my path."

When life is hectic and overwhelming or simply chock full of good, God-oriented things, we need direction. We need to be reminded of our purpose and of our calling as followers of Christ. God's Word should always be the true north on our compass.

3. Matthew 6:20

"...lay up for yourselves treasures in heaven, where neither moth nor rust destroys and where thieves do not break in and steal."

The longer we neglect our relationship with the Lord, the easier it is to forget where our true treasure lies. For our eyes to be focused on heaven, our hearts must be focused on HIM. It is only then that we can let go of worldly pleasures and live with anticipation to the heavenly joys that await us.

4. James 4:7

"Submit yourselves therefore to God. Resist the devil, and he will flee from you."

The enemy wants us to be distracted and to spend less time in fellowship with the Lord. When we give in to the distractions of this world, we are much more likely to give in to other temptations as well. In order to fight temptation, we need to be in step with the Spirit and have the Word fresh in our hearts and minds.

5. 2 Thessalonians 3:16

"Now may the Lord of peace himself give you peace at all times in every way. The Lord be with you all."

One way the Lord lavishes his love on us is by giving us peace. We can have peace on easy days as well as during the most turbulent times. Yet, when we neglect our time with the Lord, we find ourselves feeling anxious, irritable and distant. It amazes me that even though I know this, I still often choose chaos over the peace of God.

6. 2 Corinthians 13:11

"Finally, brothers, rejoice. Aim for restoration, comfort one another, agree with one another, live in peace; and the God of love and peace will be with you."

I've noticed a pattern that arises when I'm not actively seeking the Lord. I am not quick to rejoice; I'm quick to grumble. I find myself not aiming for restoration, but justifying broken relationships. I am not agreeable; I argue. And I do not live in peace. I cause upheaval. In other words, neglecting my time with the Lord is like any other sin – it doesn't just affect me, it affects those around me too.

7. John 14:27

"Peace I leave with you; my peace I give to you. Not as the world gives do I give to you. Let not your hearts be troubled, neither let them be afraid."

Our troubles and fears seem farther away when we're constantly resting in the Father's arms. But as soon as we step away and direct our focus on earthly things, those same troubles and fears move from the back burner to front and center. He longs to see us rest in his peace and to have our focus on him. He is the source of our peace.

Encouragement

Life is busy and the thought of personal soul care can seem daunting. Just as we sometimes tire of investing in our friendships and marriages, the same can happen in our relationship with the Lord. Relationships take work and we are quick to forget the benefits of putting in the effort.

When we are drenched in God's Word, when we meditate on the deep love he has for us and we pause to reflect on all he has, is and will do for us, we will, by the power of the Holy Spirit, respond in love. It is this love between the Father and his child that gives us a longing to be in his presence and care for our souls.

- **He will renew your strength**

Isaiah 40:30-31 tells us that, *"Even youths shall faint and be weary, and young men shall fall exhausted; but they who wait for the Lord shall renew their strength; they shall mount up with wings like eagles; they shall run and not be weary; they shall walk and not faint."*

Sometimes I neglect my time with the Lord because I'm busy and distracted but sometimes it's because I'm weary. Counseling can be physically, emotionally, and spiritually draining. But this is not the time to be lazy with our spiritual disciplines. This is the time to draw closer to the Lord, to lean in and dig into his Word. He will meet you in your weariness and he will renew your strength.

- **He lets us know him**

I love the sweet simplicity of John 10:14, *"I am the good shepherd. I know my own and my own know me."*

We know God because he has opened the eyes of our hearts and allowed us to know him, but our knowing him can and should be more than a surface level knowing. He not only allows us, but invites us to know him intimately. Spend time with him, talk with him, walk with him, meditate on his word. His word is life and it is yours. Strive to know him as intimately as he knows you.

- **He is the source of all we need**

Psalm 23 tells us,

> *"The Lord is my shepherd; I shall not want. He makes me lie down in green pastures. He leads me beside still waters. He restores my soul. He leads me in paths of righteousness for his name's sake. Even though I walk through the valley of the shadow of death, I will fear no evil, for you are with me; your rod and your staff, they comfort me. You prepare a table before me in the presence of my enemies; you anoint my head with oil; my cup overflows. Surely goodness and mercy shall follow me all the days of my life, and I shall dwell in the house of the Lord forever."*

This psalm is the epitome of encouragement, but when we neglect our time with the Lord, we're quick to forget these things. He leads us, restores us, abides with us, and comforts us. Our cups overflow with his love and mercy. And as if all these promises aren't enough, we will dwell in the house of the Lord forever. Let us dwell on these words. May these truths penetrate our hearts and lead us to deeper love, worship and devotion to our heavenly Father.

Personal Reflections

1. What is your daily routine for spending time with the Lord for your own spiritual growth?

2. What are the distractions in your life that lure you away from alone time with God?

3. What steps have you taken, or perhaps need to take, to be more disciplined in this area?

4. Describe a time when you neglected time with the Lord and it affected a counseling session.

5. How would you explain the importance of personal soul care to a counselee who neglects spiritual disciplines?

6. What does it mean to you to be still and know he is God?

Chapter 7

Spiritual Warfare

The enemy will not see you vanish into God's company without an effort to reclaim you.

C.S. Lewis

Veronica came to me for counseling to deal with some pretty significant body image issues. She had developed some unhealthy eating habits in order to maintain her ideal weight and as a result her body was not functioning properly. She was frustrated, scared and discouraged. The good news was that she understood her thinking was faulty and she accepted responsibility for her sinful behavior. Veronica wanted to change and was eager to see the work of the Holy Spirit in her life.

Our time together was enjoyable. Veronica was kind and sensitive. In fact she always prayed for me after I prayed for her at the close of our sessions. I truly looked forward to our time together each week as her sweet spirit was an encouragement to me. There was, however, something unique about Veronica. She was always happy to do whatever homework assignment I gave her, but she would often give *me* homework.

Veronica spent a lot of time in the Word but she had a hard time applying the truths to her life. We quickly realized that was, in part, because she was easily confused by what appeared to be contradictions in the Word. She was disciplined to be in the Word but she had not been taught how to dig into commentaries or to view individual scriptures in their greater context. So, she made a habit of bringing in a list of scriptures that confused her from her reading that week and asking if I would show her how to find their greater context and convince her that the Word was not faulty or contradicting itself. I always made time for this, because after all, biblical counseling is a form of discipleship, so I wasn't going to tell her to take her biblical confusion elsewhere; I was happy to help. And this was a good opportunity for me to learn more as well.

Because there was so much to cover in our hour session, I didn't want this to take up the bulk of our time. Therefore I would do some research on my own during the week and then walk her through it during a portion of our time together, showing her the resources I used and how to utilize them. This worked well, and I enjoyed not only the challenge but also watching her make connections and see her joy in getting answers to her questions. But over time something unexpected happened. I started doubting the very truths I was trying to convince Veronica of.

As I sat with my Bible, commentaries and online resources I found myself digging into the Word with a new found zeal. I was excited to be helping Veronica in this way and I anticipated God teaching me some new things as well. But as I dug in, dissected and meditated on the words before me, I started having an internal dialog that was a bit unsettling. If you're familiar with the Lord of the Rings series, you'll know what I mean when I compare myself to Gollum. I wasn't bent over a pool of water talking to my reflection, but I was talking to myself as if there were two of me. Here's an example of what you would have heard had you been in my head.

"This is crazy. Who actually believes this?"

"I do. I believe this."

"Do you though? Really? This is like reading any of your fiction books. It's just another story."

"No, it isn't. All other stories point to this story. And yes, I believe it."

"Do you though?"

"Yes."

"Really? This is ludicrous, admit it."

"No it isn't. This is the inspired Word of God. Nothing about this is ludicrous."

"Really? You know how ridiculous this sounds, right? No one in their right mind would believe this."

"You're wrong. It's not ridiculous. I mean, sure, it sounds ridiculous if you're not a child of God. But I am. So, it's not ridiculous.``

"Are you a child of God? Or do you just think you are?"

"I am. I know I am."

"How do you know? How do you know *this* isn't the deception?"

"Because I know."

"Do you?"

"I think so. Yes. Yes I do. I think."

"You think or you know?"

"I think I know."

"Hmmm…"

"I don't want to talk about this anymore."

There were a variety of these internal conversations and they usually ended with me closing my Bible, pushing my laptop out of reach and walking away wringing my hands. It would have been enough to have just had these conversations going on inside, but that's not all that was happening. I would get a physical coldness, a restlessness and an uneasy feeling. The entire experience was so unsettling that I didn't want to open my Bible because I didn't want this to keep happening. It made sense in the moment that if studying God's Word made me feel unsettled, then clearly I should stop reading God's Word. I can tell you now, that's absolutely *not* the right thing to do.

Don't worry, my pulling away from the Lord didn't last long. In fact, I quickly put into practice what I would teach a counselee in this situation. When I found myself hesitating to be in the Word, I would speak truth to myself by reminding myself of God's faithfulness. In order to convince myself that *this* was not the deception, I would think through my testimony and remind myself of how my eyes were opened. *This* was no deception, I would tell myself. This was spiritual warfare.

As I would pray and ask God to shut the mouth of the other voice in my head, I would also ask the Spirit to illuminate the scriptures for me and to take away any doubt that might arise. What often came to my mind during this time was Mark 9:14-24. Here we are given the account of a father who is seeking healing for his son. The man approaches Jesus and explains that his son has a spirit that makes him mute. It often seizes him and throws him into the fire or water trying to destroy him. This father is desperate! He took his son to the disciples to cast this spirit out and they were not able, so here he is begging Jesus to do this miraculous thing and save his son. Jesus says to the man, *"All things are possible for one who believes."* Then verse 24 tells us, *"Immediately the father of the child cried out and said, 'I believe; help my unbelief!'"*

In those moments when I would force myself to open God's Word, I would echo this father's cry, "I believe! Help me with my unbelief!" This was perhaps the first time I had ever experienced what we see described in Ephesians 6:12, *"For we do not wrestle against flesh and blood, but against the rulers, against the authorities, against the cosmic powers over this present darkness, against the spiritual forces of evil in the heavenly places."* This was more than my sinful flesh pulling me away. In fact, my habit in those moments - when fighting against my own flesh and blood - was to recite a line from *Come, Thou Fount of Every Blessing*. I would say aloud, "Prone to wander, Lord, I feel it, prone to leave the God I love. Here's my heart, oh, take and seal it, seal it for thy courts above."[17]

While this beloved hymn still rang true, I felt for the first time that I was being awakened to the realities of the spiritual realm. It wasn't enough to acknowledge that I'm prone to leave the God I love because I felt a tug from something more than myself. My thoughts were being distorted and challenged in a way I had never experienced before. All I knew to do was cry out, "I believe. Help me with my unbelief!" I also found myself singing *A Mighty Fortress Is Our God*, and I can't help but assume the Holy Spirit was bringing this to mind.

> And though this world, with devils filled, should threaten to undo us,
> We will not fear, for God hath willed his truth to triumph through us.
> The Prince of Darkness grim,— We tremble not for him;
> His rage we can endure, For lo! his doom is sure,—
> One little word shall fell him.[18]

This hymn was the reassurance I needed. Yes, this world is devil filled and he does threaten to undo us. But, we don't have to fear, for God is the victor! Satan's doom is sure! And while there is debate on what Luther meant by "One little word shall fell him," I've heard it said that that one little word is "Jesus." Praise God, he allowed his Spirit to give me the confidence to cling to Jesus. He was, and is, my fortress. He is my rock and my salvation! He is my shelter in the storm. He is my

---

[17] Robert Robinson, "Come, Thou Fount of Every Blessing," 1758.
[18] Martin Luther, "A Mighty Fortress Is Our God," ca. 1529.

everything! So, to him I ran. To him I cried out, "I believe; help me with my unbelief!"

While these attacks from the enemy took me by surprise and were shocking in their own way, I knew to expect spiritual warfare. I knew this the same way my husband and I knew to warn our youngest son of spiritual warfare when he chose to go to college for pastoral ministries. And in the same way, my husband and I prepared ourselves for spiritual warfare when he became an elder in our church. So, in case no one has warned you yet, *you* should expect spiritual warfare. Why? Because the enemy doesn't want you counseling people from God's Word. He wants you to doubt what you hold true. He wants you to feel so unsettled by those internal conversations that you close your Bible, walk away, and decide the best course of action is to avoid God altogether. Satan is crafty and he hates God; he doesn't want any of us utilizing His Word. He wants to foil any plans of the Holy Spirit to bring about change in the lives of our counselees. He wants us to doubt God, not trust him. He wants us to hate God, not love him. He wants us to believe that our Bible is just another book worthy of collecting dust on the shelf rather than what it is: a lamp to our feet and a light to our path.

When I was younger, I thought that spiritual warfare was reserved for the super Christian. You know - pastors, missionaries or the biblical counselor. But the truth is we are all, as Christ followers, subject to the schemes of the enemy. In fact, I've heard it said that if you claim to be a Christian and have never experienced spiritual warfare, you might want to take inventory of your spiritual disciplines. The idea is that when we are drawing near to Christ, the enemy is trying to pull us away. So if you never experience that tug pulling you away from Christ, perhaps you are not as close to him as you think you are. Robert Murray McCheyne, a Scottish minister in the 1800s, is known for saying, "I know well that when Christ is nearest, Satan also is busiest."

In his book *Desiring God,* John Piper says,

> *Satan's number one objective is to destroy our faith. We have one offensive weapon: the sword of the Spirit, the Word of God (Eph 6:17). But what many Christians fail to realize is that we can't draw the sword from someone else's scabbard. If we don't wear it, we can't wield it. If the Word of God does not abide in us (Jn. 15:7), we will reach for it in vain when the enemy strikes. But if we do wear it, if it lives within us, what mighty warriors we can be!*[19]

By the work of the Holy Spirit, I decided to be a mighty warrior and face this spiritual warfare head on. The first thing I did was talk to my husband. He is the head of my home and by the work of the Spirit in him, I knew I could trust his insight and count on him to help pray me through this situation. The second thing I did was inform the elders of my church body and ask them also to pray for me. My third step was to confide in some close girlfriends whom I knew wouldn't take this lightly. I knew they would cover me in prayer, check in on me and offer encouragement. Then, last but not least, I prepared my mind as we are encouraged to do in 1 Peter 1:13: *"Preparing your minds for action, and being sober-minded, set your hope fully on the grace that will be brought to you at the revelation of Jesus Christ."*

How exactly do we prepare our minds for action? What came to my mind was Ephesians 6:13-18.

> *Therefore take up the whole armor of God, that you may be able to withstand in the evil day, and having done all, to stand firm.*

---

[19] John Piper, *Desiring God: Meditations of a Christian Hedonist* (Sisters, Oregon: Questar Publishers, Inc., 1996), 129.

Stand therefore, having fastened on the belt of truth, and having put on the breastplate of righteousness, and, as shoes for your feet, having put on the readiness given by the gospel of peace. In all circumstances take up the shield of faith, with which you can extinguish all the flaming darts of the evil one; and take the helmet of salvation, and the sword of the Spirit, which is the word of God, praying at all times in the Spirit, with all prayer and supplication. To that end, keep alert with all perseverance, making supplication for all the saints.

What I want to focus on here is the shield of faith. In Paul's day, soldiers carried a shield that was wooden on the inside but on the outside, facing the enemy, it was covered in a metal plate and then on top of that was a layer of leather. This design was intended to stop a sword or knife at close range and an arrow, whether they be flaming or not, from longer ranges. When soldiers stood side by side, the barrier they created with these shields was virtually impenetrable. Having faith in the promises of God can protect us in the same way.

God never promised us health, financial freedom, stress-free lives or protection from spiritual warfare. What God does promise is that he will never leave us or forsake us. He promises that, through the death of Jesus Christ, we are forgiven. He has promised that through the seal of the Holy Spirit we are guaranteed our inheritance. These are the very promises the enemy wants us to doubt. He wants us to question the validity of these promises and convince us that they weren't meant for us. But when we hold to these promises as a shield, the flaming darts of the enemy can't penetrate us. We may feel the arrows hit and our shield may shake or shift; we may feel the heat of the flames and question if we're strong enough to withstand the attack. We may be frightened, discouraged and even wonder if it's worth the effort.

But God.

Not only can we trust God to keep his promises, we can trust him to give us the strength we need to hold that shield with confidence. We can trust that he will uphold us when we're tempted to waver and he will give us a way out when we're tempted to give up. Notice Paul tells us to pray at all times. I believe in the power of prayer, 100%. I hope you noticed that my first line of defense against spiritual warfare was to ask my husband, elders, and trusted friends to join me in prayer. But now that we've talked about the shield of faith, which is a defensive weapon, let's look at the sword of the Spirit, which is the Word of God, an offensive weapon.

In chapter 6 we discussed the importance of personal soul care and how that starts with being in the Word. Knowing the Word, having it written in our hearts and ready to flow from our mouths is how we go on the offense in our battle against the enemy. We see this example played out by Jesus himself in Matthew 4 when he was tempted by Satan in the wilderness. What did Jesus do when faced with temptation? He quoted scripture! This, my friends, is the sword of the Spirit.

Let's revisit Moses and the Israelites and look at their own battle with spiritual warfare. If you'll remember, in Exodus 24:12 the Lord said to Moses, *"Come up to me on the mountain and wait there, that I may give you the tablets of stone, with the law and the commandment, which I have written for their instruction."* We see starting in verse 15 that Moses did as the Lord asked.

> *Then Moses went up on the mountain, and the cloud covered the mountain. The glory of the Lord dwelt on Mount Sinai, and the cloud covered it six days. And on the seventh day he called to Moses out of the midst of the cloud. Now the appearance of the glory of the Lord was like a devouring fire on the top of the mountain in the sight of the people of Israel. Moses entered the*

cloud and went up on the mountain. And Moses was on the mountain forty days and forty nights.

The Lord gave Moses a LOT of information during those 40 days and 40 nights. We can read about it over the next eight chapters, but I want to draw your attention to what we find in chapter 32. Read with me from verses 1 - 10.

When the people saw that Moses delayed to come down from the mountain, the people gathered themselves together to Aaron and said to him, "Up, make us gods who shall go before us. As for this Moses, the man who brought us up out of the land of Egypt, we do not know what has become of him." So Aaron said to them, "Take off the rings of gold that are in the ears of your wives, your sons, and your daughters, and bring them to me." So all the people took off the rings of gold that were in their ears and brought them to Aaron. And he received the gold from their hand and fashioned it with a graving tool and made a golden calf. And they said, "These are your gods, O Israel, who brought you up out of the land of Egypt!" When Aaron saw this, he built an altar before it. And Aaron made a proclamation and said, "Tomorrow shall be a feast to the Lord." And they rose up early the next day and offered burnt offerings and brought peace offerings. And the people sat down to eat and drink and rose up to play.

And the Lord said to Moses, "Go down, for your people, whom you brought up out of the land of Egypt, have corrupted themselves. They have turned aside quickly out of the way that I commanded them. They have made for themselves a golden calf and have worshiped it and sacrificed to it and said, 'These are your gods, O Israel, who brought you up out of the land of Egypt!'" And the Lord said to Moses, "I have seen this people, and behold, it is a stiff-necked people. Now therefore let me alone,

that my wrath may burn hot against them and I may consume
them, in order that I may make a great nation of you."

Remember who we're reading about. These are the same people who were rescued from slavery. They watched the waters part before their eyes to give them safe passage and then they saw their enemy swallowed up by those same waters. These people grumbled and yet the Lord provided water and food for them. These people saw God in action. They saw the Lord go before them as a cloud to guide them by day and as fire by night to light their path. These people saw incredible things. Things that should shake a man to his core and change him forever! Yet, what happens when 40 days have passed and they're tired of waiting on Moses to return? I'm shaking my head in disbelief as I type these words. . . they made a golden calf and worshiped it.

Why am I shaking my head at this? Because it's crazy? Yes. But also because I see myself in these people. I don't share the same experiences as the Israelites but I've seen the Lord do some pretty incredible things in my life. I could write a book on the ways I've seen the Spirit protect me, guide me, prompt me and interact with me. I've had experiences that should have shaken me to my core and changed me forever. And what did I do the moment I started doubting God's Word? I walked away. Just as the natural inclination of the Israelites was to forget God and replace him, my natural inclination was to give stock to the doubts and questions the enemy was feeding me. I'm willing to bet this is your natural inclination too.

Prone to wander Lord I feel it, prone to leave the God I love...

Let's continue reading verses 11-14.

But Moses implored the Lord his God and said, "O Lord, why
does your wrath burn hot against your people, whom you have
brought out of the land of Egypt with great power and with a

mighty hand? Why should the Egyptians say, 'With evil intent did he bring them out, to kill them in the mountains and to consume them from the face of the earth'? Turn from your burning anger and relent from this disaster against your people. Remember Abraham, Isaac, and Israel, your servants, to whom you swore by your own self, and said to them, 'I will multiply your offspring as the stars of heaven, and all this land that I have promised I will give to your offspring, and they shall inherit it forever.'" And the Lord relented from the disaster that he had spoken of bringing on his people.

We serve a just God who has every right to burn with anger against his people. But God is also kind, compassionate and long suffering. Just as he showed mercy by relenting from the disaster that he had threatened to bring on the Isrealites, he showed mercy to me by allowing his Spirit to minister to my soul. He gave me the strength and conviction I needed to approach him in boldness and ask for help. He gave me the strength and courage I needed to reopen my Bible day after day and fight to quiet the voices in my head that whispered deceit. He reminded me of his faithfulness, not only to his people throughout the generations, but to me personally. He walked me through the spiritual warfare, he used it as part of my sanctification and as a result, he increased my faith. I have every confidence he will do the same for you.

Here's my heart, Oh take and seal it, seal it for thy courts above...

What's in your Toolbox?

Spiritual warfare will not only be a reality for you, but also for your counselees. It's imperative that we're prepared. I often think of my grandfather, who drove a tank in the 7th Armored Division in World War II. I not only have the flag my grandmother was presented when he died, but I also have the small, tattered New Testament that he carried in his breast pocket while in uniform. Imagine yourself stepping onto the battlefield. What truths in that tattered Bible would bring you, or your counselee, the most comfort and give you the most courage to face your enemy?

1.   Romans 8:35-39

"Who shall separate us from the love of Christ? Shall tribulation, or distress, or persecution, or famine, or nakedness, or danger, or sword? As it is written, 'For your sake we are being killed all the day long; we are regarded as sheep to be slaughtered.' No, in all these things we are more than conquerors through him who loved us. For I am sure that neither death nor life, nor angels nor rulers, nor things present nor things to come, nor powers, nor height nor depth, nor anything else in all creation, will be able to separate us from the love of God in Christ Jesus our Lord."

What an amazing truth to know the enemy can throw everything he has at us, but we will never be his. As children of God, we are HIS and nothing - nothing - can separate us from his love! We can face any battle that comes our way knowing that HE has won the war!

2. Psalm 28:7

"The LORD is my strength and my shield; in him my heart trusts, and I am helped; my heart exults, and with my song I give thanks to him."

It's difficult to give thanks in the middle of spiritual warfare, but that's exactly what we can do! With the Spirit of God dwelling in us we can trust him wholly to be our strength and shield. Knowing the love the Father has for us and the sacrifice his son, Jesus Christ, made on our behalf, we can face any foe with a song of thanksgiving on our tongue!

3. Joshua 1:9

"Have I not commanded you? Be strong and courageous. Do not be frightened, and do not be dismayed, for the Lord your God is with you wherever you go."

We don't know when the enemy will attack and when we'll find ourselves battling the spiritual realm, so I pray it brings you hope and comfort to know that whether we are at the grocery store, story hour, in a nursing home or in the counseling room, the Lord God is with us. We can stand strong and courageous in the face of our enemy because he is with us every step of the way.

4. John 16:33

"I have said these things to you, that in me you may have peace. In the world you will have tribulation. But take heart; I have overcome the world."

Fighting spiritual battles under the care of our worldly leaders would be a disaster. We would face our enemy with the realization that our commander in chief is just as weak as we are. Praise God that's not our situation! We fight our spiritual battles under the care of the One who has already overcome the world. We serve the Sovereign One who created everything. It is all his and in him we can have peace.

5. Psalm 18:6

"In my distress I called upon the Lord; to my God I cried for help. From his temple he heard my voice, and my cry to him reached his ears."

When spiritual battles come, and they will, we can rest assured that he knows. He is not blind to our trials nor is he deaf to our cries. He hears us when we call out for help and he is ever ready to deliver us from the enemy.

6. 2 Thessalonians 3:3-5

"But the Lord is faithful. He will establish you and guard you against the evil one. And we have confidence in the Lord about you, that you are doing and will do the things that we command. May the Lord direct your hearts to the love of God and to the steadfastness of Christ."

Often when faced with spiritual warfare, we stand on the battlefield, turn to look for backup and see ourselves standing there alone. We shrink as we realize that no one is coming to our aid. Why are we so quick to envision this for ourselves when it couldn't be further from the truth. God is faithful! As his children we can have confidence that he will establish us and guard us against the evil one. Never are we on the battlefield alone.

7. Nahum 1:7

"The Lord is good, a stronghold in the day of trouble; he knows those who take refuge in him."

Saying the Lord is good is not a statement about what he does. It is a statement about who he is. HE IS GOOD. We can take refuge in him and know that he will not betray us and turn us over to the enemy. He is our stronghold. He is not only our best defense, but our only defense.

Encouragement

As you think about past, present or future bouts of spiritual warfare, imagine your Heavenly Father looking on with love and compassion, giving you a way out of any temptation that might be rearing its ugly head. Imagine Jesus advocating for you and the Holy Spirit praying for you when you, yourself, can't find the words.

What a beautiful, calming picture in the midst of a raging battle. Praise God this beautiful calm is our reality. We are not alone when the enemy seeks to destroy us. May you find encouragement in the Word and through the work of the Holy Spirit and may you have the foresight to dress yourself each morning in the full armor of God.

- **He is greater**

1 John 4:4 says, *"Little children, you are from God and have overcome them, for he who is in you is greater than he who is in the world."*

When faced with spiritual warfare we're reminded of how strong, crafty and captivating the enemy can be. It is then, regardless of our age, that we feel helpless like little children. Yet, our God is greater! We can stand firm, even as little children, because we are his and he has overcome the world!

- **He values you**

Matthew 10:29-31 is such a great reminder of God's love for us. It says, *"Are not two sparrows sold for a penny? And not one of them will fall to the ground apart from your Father. But even the hairs of your head are all numbered. Fear not, therefore; you are of more value than many sparrows."*

It's easy in the middle of spiritual warfare to feel alone and forgotten. We often wonder where God is and ask why he's turned his back on us. But we must remember he knows us intimately and loves us more than we can even comprehend. We should take great comfort in knowing how much he loves and values us.

- **He will give you rest**

Matthew 11:28 perfectly describes the Father's heart towards us, *"Come to me, all who labor and are heavy laden, and I will give you rest."*

Spiritual warfare is no small thing. It can leave us feeling empty and exhausted. Praise God that he doesn't leave us on our own when we need to be refreshed and replenished. He invites us to come to him for rest. Take a moment to praise him for the fact that he protects us, fights for us, and still offers *us* rest. What a kind and merciful God we serve.

Personal Reflections

1. Write about a time when you faced spiritual warfare. Take time to reflect on the counselees you were seeing at the time. Write about any correlations you see between the type of spiritual warfare you experienced and the cases you were handling at the time.

2. Write out a plan for yourself in preparation for future spiritual battles. Include successful strategies from past experiences as well as things you would do differently.

3. How would you encourage a counselee in the midst of spiritual warfare to draw closer to the Lord rather than pull away?

4. Thinking through the armor of God, which piece of armor do you gravitate to in times of trouble? Why do you think this is so?

5. We all have hearts that are prone to wander. What strongholds does the enemy have over you that tend to pull you away from abiding in Christ?

6. What steps do you think we can take as Christians to help our wandering hearts wander less often?

Chapter 8

The Temptation to Gossip

Make the mule of your tongue serve the mercy of your heart.

John Piper

Not long after I started meeting with Marcy, mutual friends started coming to me saying, "Marcy said you guys were meeting for counseling. That's so great. She really needs help and you're the right person for the job." I would smile and say something along the lines of, "I'm glad she's got you to talk to. You're a good friend." This type of interaction went on for a while but then something shifted. Marcy realized what I already knew, that she wanted her problems to go away, but her heart was hard and she wasn't ready to repent of her sin and do the work of putting off and putting on. In her realization of this, she decided biblical counseling wasn't going to work and she informed me that not only would we not continue meeting, but that she would be pursuing secular counseling. She wanted someone who would help her feel better, not help her face her sin.

With sadness, I released her from my care and prayed that the Lord would soften her heart and open her eyes to the life-changing help available through God's Word. What do you think happened next? Those same mutual friends, who were once so encouraging, were now coming to me saying, "Oh, I'm so sorry to hear that you and Marcy aren't meeting anymore. She said it didn't work. She's going to try meeting with someone else. A secular counselor. Maybe she'll have better luck with them." I couldn't see in the hearts of these individuals, but what my ears heard was a disappointment in not only me and my ability to counsel, but an accusation that biblical counseling as a whole wasn't helpful.

Perhaps you have faced a situation similar to this. Every inch of my being wanted to defend myself, what I do, and more importantly, the reputation of God's Word. I wanted to point out that God's Word didn't fail Marcy, her hard heart did. What I wanted to do in that moment was to break Marcy's confidence and help these friends understand what was really going on. I wanted to give them examples of her struggles and how I pointed her to the Word and then how she rejected that truth. I wanted to give them an accurate picture of how messed up Marcy's thinking was so that they would understand she was the problem, not me. Have you ever felt the need to defend yourself and the counsel you've given someone?

I spoke about this recently with my friend and co-laborer, Marilyn. She worked as a nurse for over thirty years and can see some great parallels to her job then as a nurse and her position now as a biblical counselor.

> *As a pediatric emergency room nurse in an inner city hospital, we had some very hard days. Babies brought in by police and social workers, abused children, situations of domestic violence, drugs, sexual assault and murder. Situations that would be on the front page of the morning newspaper the next day. Often the newspaper report was so inaccurately depicted, those of us who were present in the situation would shake our heads and wonder how the reporting could be so far off the mark. Yet, no matter how outrageous the*

*account, we could never comment or even hint that we knew
anything about the circumstances.*

*How does this apply to biblical counseling? In order for a counselee
to trust me as her counselor, she must know that I will respect her
privacy and her right to confidentiality wherever possible. Recently,
a counselee said through tears, "It's not easy to come here and talk
to you about these things. It's embarrassing and hard." Another
said, "I've never talked to anyone about this before. I didn't know
it was inside of me." This puts the burden on us as counselors to
protect that confidentiality not only through action but also
appearance. Gossip is an ugly word and the Bible speaks strongly
against it.*

Perhaps you've never faced a situation where you felt the urge to break
a confidence in the name of defending yourself. But what about good
old fashioned gossip? We had a friend many years ago who was also a
nurse, and he loved telling stories about the patients he would see. The
gorier the injury the better. The more shocking the details the more
animated he became. If a body part was doing something it wasn't
intended to do, the harder he laughed. And of course, the more his
crowd reacted, the more stories he told. He was careful not to use
names, or any personal information, but he loved creating the suspense
that we might actually know some of these people. After all, we live in a
small town surrounded by other small towns. This did two things for
me. One, I quickly made up my mind that, should I ever have an
emergency, I would never go to the hospital where he worked. Two, I
knew if I wanted a good story, which likely was an exaggerated version
of the truth, this was the guy to go to.

We all love to hear a good story and most of us like being the one
telling it, and as biblical counselors we've got an endless supply of

stories. Even so, we should never catch ourselves listening to our counselee and thinking about who would enjoy this story, who would laugh the hardest or who would take in the deepest gasp. We not only have to resist the temptation to gossip, we also have to see our counselee's words as *more* than stories. We have to remember that what we're being trusted with is a person's heartache, a longing, a wound, a fear. We have to handle the information given to us with love, compassion, care and concern. We need to be worthy of the trust our counselees are putting in us. There are times, yes, when confidentiality has to be broken and church leadership and perhaps even the authorities have to be apprised of a situation. There are times when information is shared with another counselor or pastor in order to obtain advice. But with the exception of those (hopefully) rare occasions, our counselees have to know they are safe to talk freely with us and that they are there for our help, not our amusement.

I told you that Marilyn was a nurse for over thirty years. She recently retired as a flight nurse serving in the Yukon, so as you can imagine, she has some amazing stories, but never have I seen her work for a laugh or a reaction of shock and awe at the expense of her patients. In fact, the stories I've heard from her are about the loving community of people and the breathtaking scenery, not about the intense work she did there. This is how we must see our counselees - as people. As image bearers. As brothers and sisters in Christ whose lives and life circumstances are precious to the Lord and therefore should be precious to us. For our counselees who have yet to trust in the Lord, they too are God's creation and are to be considered with as much love and compassion as anyone else. I pray gossiping about your counselees has never been a temptation, but if it has, ask the Lord to keep that temptation far from you. Ask God to give you eyes to see your counselees as he sees them. Remember these wise words from Marilyn.

So many of our counselees are struggling with a lack of faith especially in the early days of counseling. It's also important to remember that struggling people are vulnerable and often hypersensitive, less ready to trust, especially when they may have just told you some very personal details about their struggles.

Getting caught up in gossip about your counselee is not only sinful but potentially devastating. A little over twenty years ago I was seeing a counselor that was on staff at the church we were attending. I was also on staff at the church, as a secretary, and one day a fellow staff member mentioned something to me that I had been struggling with. Their concern was genuine, but the problem was that I had only ever voiced this concern to my counselor. I knew instantly that my confidence had been broken. This was not a matter that warranted the attention of the elders or anyone else for that matter. This was a simple case of me being gossiped about by my counselor. I was young, young in my faith, and a newlywed. I had sought counseling to process through some significant trust issues that had come about by someone else's sin against me and then my counselor repeated something I had said during a session. Did you catch that? I went to counseling because I had significant trust issues and then my counselor gossiped about me with a fellow coworker. This was not only a major setback in my growth and healing, but it took years for me to be willing to see another counselor.

As we've already seen, gossip can come about in many different forms. What about unintentional gossip? I suppose one could argue that this isn't really gossip, but the principle is the same. Our words can be used for life or death. Sometimes our words are misused with intentionality, and sometimes not. Let's look at an example of this from Marilyn.

I have a counselee who referred a friend to me. They know I meet with both of them the same weekday yet one will always ask if I'm meeting her friend that day. Added to that, she often comments, "I hope you're meeting with her today. She had a bad night and a tough morning." This is a potential pitfall for you as a counselor. It's too easy to take the bait, especially since none of us want to appear rude.

Perhaps you have found yourself in a similar circumstance. Have you felt tongue-tied trying not to say too much but just enough not to seem rude? I have found that counseling is a breeding ground for awkward situations, inside and outside the counseling room. Gossip can be born out of intentionality and out of carelessness. Read Proverbs 15:28 with me. *"The heart of the righteous ponders how to answer, but the mouth of the wicked pours out evil things."* Whether it's good old-fashioned gossip or an unexpected pitfall, we need to be in the habit of pondering our words before they leave our mouths. Let's also consider the wisdom found in Proverbs 17:27. *"Whoever restrains his words has knowledge, and he who has a cool spirit is a man of understanding."* This verse echoes the truth from the previous one. Sometimes we are a bit too eager to respond, when it would be more prudent to stop and ponder, to let our spirit, so to speak, cool off.

Another form of gossip to consider is when you, as the counselor, are gossiped about. Have you had your words, spoken in love to a counselee, get twisted and repeated back to you from someone else out of context and in a tone that completely changed your original intent? It's these moments that can leave you feeling alone and misunderstood. It's these moments that can tempt you to correct the gossip, explain the context and thereby break the confidence of your counselee. This is when we hold our tongues and address the matter privately with our counselee. But what if the counselee doesn't go back and correct the other people? How many people are you now misrepresented to? These questions can go on and on and become all consuming. This is when discouragement can creep in and leave you wondering why you ever wanted to do this in the first place. Marilyn has some good reminders to share with us.

> *The counseling session needs to be a safe place for the counselee to speak with you, the counselor. Some counselees are quite comfortable sharing their experience with family and friends but others are not. The counselee has the right to talk about her counseling with anyone she chooses. She can be as specific as she wishes. She can share the advice you've given her. It's entirely possible that her account of your words might be different from what you said or intended. It's not for you to respond to what you hear lest it be from a source of gossip. Depending on the subject matter and extent of the gossip, it may be appropriate to discuss this with your counselee. She may not realize how her words were interpreted, or she may not understand some of what you said during the previous session.*

Let's revisit Moses and the Israelites to be reminded of the dangerous consequences of slander and gossip. We'll be reading Numbers 12:1-15.

> *Miriam and Aaron spoke against Moses because of the Cushite woman whom he had married, for he had married a Cushite woman. And they said, "Has the Lord indeed spoken only through Moses? Has he not spoken through us also?" And the Lord heard it. Now the man Moses was very meek, more than all people who were on the face of the earth. And suddenly the Lord said to Moses and to Aaron and Miriam, "Come out, you three, to the tent of meeting." And the three of them came out. And the Lord came down in a pillar of cloud and stood at the entrance of the tent and called Aaron and Miriam, and they both came forward. And he said, "Hear my words: If there is a prophet*

among you, I the Lord make myself known to him in a vision; I speak with him in a dream. Not so with my servant Moses. He is faithful in all my house. With him I speak mouth to mouth, clearly, and not in riddles, and he beholds the form of the Lord. Why then were you not afraid to speak against my servant Moses?" And the anger of the Lord was kindled against them, and he departed.

When the cloud removed from over the tent, behold, Miriam was leprous, like snow. And Aaron turned toward Miriam, and behold, she was leprous. And Aaron said to Moses, "Oh, my lord, do not punish us because we have done foolishly and have sinned. Let her not be as one dead, whose flesh is half eaten away when he comes out of his mother's womb." And Moses cried to the Lord, "O God, please heal her—please." But the Lord said to Moses, "If her father had but spit in her face, should she not be shamed seven days? Let her be shut outside the camp seven days, and after that she may be brought in again." So Miriam was shut outside the camp seven days, and the people did not set out on the march till Miriam was brought in again.

On the surface, this might seem like normal family drama. Miriam and Aaron were unhappy with Moses. They had issues with his Cushite wife. So, they spoke against him, big deal. But it *was* a big deal. Miriam was disgruntled with how Moses was leading the people and instead of holding her tongue or speaking with Moses privately, she spoke against him. The Lord heard this and his anger was kindled. Miriam, as a consequence, became leprous and thus had to be sent out of the camp for seven days. Again, this might not seem like a big deal. After all, it was customary for those with leprosy to live on the outskirts of town.

What makes this a big deal, other than the fact that all sin is a big deal, is that the Israelites were still on the move. They were headed to Canaan, the land the Lord had promised them. *This* was a big deal. And now their journey is put on hold for seven days because of Miriam's lack of control over her tongue. If you remember, in Exodus 15:20-21 we saw Miriam respond to Moses's hymn by leading the women in songs of praise focusing on the power and glory of God. Miriam, in verse 20, is called a prophetess, the first woman in the Bible to be given that rare privilege. Much later, in Micah 6:4, we are reminded of her role in the exodus of the Israelites: *"For I brought you up from the land of Egypt and redeemed you from the house of slavery, and I sent before you Moses, Aaron, and Miriam."* Miriam was no reckless, loose-lipped woman, wandering around blindly following Moses's lead. No, she was a respected, highly regarded woman.

Miriam is no different than you and I. She was serving the Lord, leading his people to the promised land. You and I are serving the Lord by leading his people through his Word by means of biblical counseling. Miriam likely let the grumblings of the people affect her attitude and she began grumbling herself. She lost sight of the goal and lost control of her tongue. If you and I aren't careful, the words of others can lead us down a similar path. We can easily lose control of our tongues in a moment of storytelling banter as well as in a moment of defending what we do. Just as Miriam's actions halted the progress of the children of Israel, we too can halt the progress of our counselees.

The Bible doesn't always give us the details of each situation. But let's think about how this might have played out. Miriam was a respectable leader among the other women and now she's been cast out of the camp with leprosy. Not because she "caught" leprosy but because she was being punished. First, imagine the danger she might have been in. A woman on the outskirts of camp all alone. It's not like they had streetlights and police patrolling the area. Second, think about the damage she did to her witness. I can just imagine the other women huddled in clumps talking about Miriam and what she had done and how she was paying the price, likely giving little regard to their own grumbling and how they, themselves, had repeatedly kindled the anger of the Lord. Imagine her homecoming. I'm sure many were happy to see her. I imagine some hugs and kind words were tossed her way. But I also imagine people staring, whispering, and holding a grudge because she had held them up. I can also see some of the women deciding they would no longer follow Miriam's lead. What kind of a woman was she, after all? The Lord had given her leprosy and shut her out of the camp! Who would follow a woman like that?

Now, let's shift the spotlight back to us, as biblical counselors. Think about the damage that could be done if we allow our tongues to go unbridled. Imagine halting the progress of a counselee who had broken decades of silence and entrusted you with her secrets. The damage would feel irreparable. What about your witness? Would people trust you, would they want to recommend you as a counselor if they knew you were prone to gossip? If you feel the need to publicly defend yourself when you're misrepresented, at the cost of breaking your counselee's confidence, how will people view your church's counseling ministry? Will they walk away saying that you are wise and humble or will they walk away saying the ministry can't be trusted?

Think about my two friends, the nurses. Both loved their jobs and were good at what they did. One looked at his job as a source of entertainment, always ready to laugh at someone else's expense. The other looked at her job as a way to preserve the dignity of those who are in vulnerable situations. Now, take these two people out of their scrubs and instead of visualizing them in a hospital, put them in the counseling room. One has a reputation for finding comic relief in the most dire circumstances. The other protects the reputation of her counselee even at the expense of her own. Which of these people would you want caring for you? Which would you feel comfortable referring others to?

Friends, we are all sinners. We will all likely fall into this trap at one point or another. None of us always has the perfect response. All of us have looked back and realized we could have handled any number of situations better. My goal is not to discourage you with thoughts of the destruction your tongue is capable of, but rather to encourage you that this temptation is real, it's okay to admit it, and there is hope. In his wisdom, God has given us instruction on how to use our tongues for life instead of death.

We know from Proverbs 18:21 that death and life are in the power of the tongue and we see this played out all around us. Tongues lead to wars and the death of marriages, churches, friendships and careers. I don't think I've ever had a counselee that *didn't* mention something hurtful that someone said to them. Think about yourself. Do you lie awake at night thinking about the weather or what you ate or drank that day? Or do you lie awake replaying conversations?

Hope is found in Proverbs 15:4. Knowing that a gentle tongue is a tree of life reminds us that our words can be used to heal marriages, strengthen churches, build friendships, and boost careers. Have you ever had a counselee thank you for encouraging her? It's heartbreaking to think you might be the only one lifting them up with your words, but you might be, and it's important to take that role seriously. It's a privilege to use our tongues to give hope to the despairing.

What else does scripture tell us about the tongue? Let's look at Luke 6:45. *"The good person out of the good treasure of his heart produces good, and the evil person out of his evil treasure produces evil, for out of the abundance of the heart his mouth speaks."* Out of the abundance of the heart, the mouth speaks. What does that tell you? It tells me that this all starts in the heart. Our ability to see our counselees as precious children of God, whose dignity we should hold dear, comes from a heart of love and compassion for others. We can resist the temptation to engage in gossip when our hearts are bent towards respecting the privacy and reputation of others. When our words have been twisted and repeated out of context, we can resist lashing back and breaking confidences if our hearts are aligned with the truth of Philippians 2:4. Putting the interests of others before our own should be the battle cry of our hearts as biblical counselors. When we live by that battle cry, our tongues can bring healing as stated in Proverbs 12:18: *"There is one whose rash words are like sword thrusts, but the tongue of the wise brings healing."*

R.C. Sproul is known for saying, "God's Word can be in the mind without being in the heart, but it cannot be in the heart without first being in the mind." As we discussed in chapter 6, being in the Word for our own spiritual growth and for the deepening of our personal relationship with the Lord must be a priority. If our hearts aren't aligned with God's Word, we won't value what he values, we won't love what he loves, and we won't protect what is worth protecting. Perhaps the Spirit has convicted you while reading this chapter. If so, take this sin to the feet of Jesus, ask for forgiveness and ask him to stand guard over your tongue as you strive to make changes.

What's in your Toolbox?

When my sons were little, a popular demonstration among the moms was to hand their child a tube of toothpaste and ask them to squeeze all the toothpaste out. Most kids jumped at this opportunity and thought it was great fun, until the mom asked them to put all the toothpaste *back* in the tube. As you can imagine, it can't be done. The parallel, of course, is that the toothpaste is like our words: once they've come out of our mouths, they can't be put back in. With this illustration in mind, let's look at more of what the Bible has to say about this.

1. Proverbs 21:23

"Whoever keeps his mouth and his tongue keeps himself out of trouble."

When the Bible says to "keep" our mouth and tongue, it is telling us to guard or protect them. We should be as mindful of our words as a shepherd is of his sheep.

2. Ephesians 4:29

"Let no corrupting talk come out of your mouths, but only such as is good for building up, as fits the occasion, that it may give grace to those who hear."

What we say or don't say in the counseling room is just as important as what we say or don't say outside the counseling room. Let's strive, by the help of the Holy Spirit, to only use our words for good, to build up and to give grace. This seems like a tall order, but with God all things are possible!

3. Proverbs 20:19

"Whoever goes about slandering reveals secrets; therefore do not associate with a simple babbler."

As Christ followers, and as biblical counselors, we want people to be drawn to us and to trust us. We must pray against the schemes of the enemy that would have us be simple babblers that should not be associated with.

4. Colossians 4:6

"Let your speech always be gracious, seasoned with salt, so that you may know how you ought to answer each person."

In the context of food, we know that salt is good for preserving, for adding flavor, and for providing nutrients. In the context of our words, we should use them to preserve the dignity of others, to draw people in (because we all want more of a good, flavorful thing), and to add goodness by building others up rather than tearing them down.

5. Matthew 15:18

"But what comes out of the mouth proceeds from the heart, and this defiles a person."

This is proof that everything we say, inside or outside the counseling room starts in our hearts. We need to be diligent in our own walk with the Lord so that our hearts will be in tune with his and that what comes out of our mouths will be evidence of that.

6. Matthew 12:36

"I tell you, on the day of judgment people will give account for every careless word they speak."

While there is no condemnation for those in Jesus Christ, we will all stand before the judgment seat and give an account for ourselves to God. Let us bridle our tongues and resist the temptation to use our words for evil so that the rewards we receive and lay at Jesus' feet will be plentiful.

7. James 1:26

"If anyone thinks he is religious and does not bridle his tongue but deceives his heart, this person's religion is worthless."

We cannot be effective in our ministry as biblical counselors or as disciplers if we do not bridle our tongue. Let's pray for ourselves and for each other that the Lord would never let it be said of us that our religion is worthless.

Encouragement

- **God desires to help you**

Matthew 7:7, "Ask, and it will be given to you; seek, and you will find; knock, and it will be opened to you."

God has invited you to ask him for help when you need it and he desires to help you! Ask him. He wants to help you bridle your tongue. He longs to align your heart with his. He desires you to be more like his Son and for your words to be lifegiving. He will help you. You only need to ask.

- **He will guard your mouth**

Psalm 141:3, "Set a guard, O LORD, over my mouth; keep watch over the door of my lips!"

There is so much comfort in knowing you can specifically ask God to stand guard over your mouth. And why wouldn't you ask for that? Having El Shaddai (God Almighty) keep watch over the door of your lips seems like the best way to ensure your words are life giving!

- **Through the Holy Spirit, self-control is possible**

Galatians 5:22-23, "But the fruit of the Spirit is love, joy, peace, forbearance, kindness, goodness, faithfulness, gentleness and self-control. Against such things there is no law."

We tend to think about self-control in the context of our sexuality or our tempers, but it applies to so many aspects of our lives, including our tongues! I have friends who joke about the gaping hole in their word filter. But as children of God, the hole in our filter can be mended. By the work of the Holy Spirit we can have control over our tongues and we can use our words to build up rather than tear down.

Personal Reflection

1. Write out your own definition of gossip and any definitions you've heard from others that differ from your own. Then list some ways that gossip harms the hearer, the teller, and the one being gossiped about.

2. When asking for advice or guidance we sometimes have to share information about our counselees with other counselors or church leadership. How do you discern if the details you share are necessary or coming from a desire to gossip?

3. Imagine being approached by someone wanting to discuss the problems of a friend they know you are counseling. Write an appropriate response to this person. How can you show kindness and interest while also protecting the privacy of your counselee?

4. Draw an image of what it might look like if we could physically see the damage being done by gossip. Looking at that image, what are some ways that damage could be undone?

5. Imagine a scenario where you, as a counselor, are being gossiped about. How do you think this potentially could affect your reputation? How do you think you would feel if your reputation was sacrificed or compromised in order to protect the privacy of your counselee?

6. How do you feel about God afflicting Miriam with leprosy after gossiping about Moses's wife? Imagine leprosy was a "side effect" of gossip today. How might that change the way you choose to speak about others?

Chapter 9

When I Feel Like a Failure

Trust the past to God's mercy, the present to God's love and the future to God's providence.

Augustine

A lesson from my junior high school years made such a lasting impression on me that it continues to resonate with me to this day. The teacher was presenting a lesson on Thomas Edison. As the story goes, he was asked by a reporter, "How did it feel to fail 1,000 times?" Edison replied, "I didn't fail 1,000 times. The light bulb was an invention with 1,000 steps." Our teacher drove home the point: failure is a part of life. We can choose to be discouraged by it and give up, or we can see it as a learning opportunity and continue moving forward.

I recognized even then that I needed to tuck those words away and carry them with me. I'm so glad I did. Failure has, indeed, been a part of my life, and I'm sure you can relate. I failed at seemingly insignificant things, like my first sewing project and my first attempt at driving a stick shift. No long term consequences resulted, but these failings sure ruffled my feathers in the moment! But I've also failed in significant, life-altering ways, like ignoring the Word of God or a prompting from the Spirit, or by being careless with my words. In some of those instances I am still, decades later, dealing with the consequences. My teacher said that failure is our friend, but it doesn't always feel that way, does it?

Have you ever felt like a failure in the counseling room? I sure have. If you haven't, I dare say you will. Two aspects of failure come to mind when I think about the counseling room. The first is when your counselee continues in sin, rejects truth and walks away leaving you *feeling* like you've failed. My friend Ashley, who was recently certified as a biblical counselor, shared a great example of this.

> *Olivia and I had been meeting together regularly and things seemed to be progressing along VERY S-L-O-W-L-Y. We had spent the majority of our time talking about the Gospel and how the Gospel transforms our daily lives. I was trying to set a good foundation to begin addressing issues of the heart. However, it was beginning to feel like each new session was "less productive" than the one before it, and it took a lot of energy to keep her on topic without our conversations getting lost in the weeds. I had a great tentative plan for moving forward and addressing the sinfulness in Olivia's life, but it was a struggle to see how our sessions were going to get to that point.*

> *A few sessions later, Olivia showed up to my office with freshly dyed blue hair and no Bible because apparently she had lost it and was not even sure where to start looking for it. She had not completed any of the previous week's homework. This was then followed by the comment, "Oh and I wanted to tell you that I have been drinking but only in my apartment so that I don't get caught." My expression must not have been very comforting because she followed with, "But at least I am not doing drugs." At this point, all I could do was pray with Olivia. I prayed for*

our time together and then continued to petition the Holy Spirit over the next hour for wisdom and guidance for myself.

A few days later I received a message from Olivia stating that she was dropping out of college and starting a full time job. She felt like her time with me had been well spent but that she would no longer have time to meet with me. We talked a bit more about this, but she was ready to move on. She felt like she had learned what she needed so that she could move forward. It was at this moment I felt I had failed!

Can you relate to this? I certainly can. In fact, Ashley and I have had multiple conversations about wayward counselees and our feelings of failure. I often equate this to parenting. We can point our children to Christ, offer them hope, show them a path to healing and a way of life that is God honoring. But there is no guarantee they will listen and put their trust in Christ. In the same way, there's no guarantee our counselee will listen, follow our counsel or walk the path of righteousness. When they do, we're elated! We rejoice and praise God! But when they don't, when they walk away and there's more work to be done, and they choose the path of destruction, our hearts break. We grieve for them. We pray for them. And then we start replaying conversations, analyzing homework assignments, questioning our abilities and whether or not we chose the best narrative. And what about the hope? Why didn't they latch on to the hope we offered from God's Word?

Do you see what happens? We start pointing a finger at ourselves, placing blame and inevitably questioning if we should even be doing this. After all, what kind of biblical counselor fails so miserably that their counselee would choose the path of darkness over the light of Jesus Christ? My hope and prayer for you is that when you find yourself in this situation you can find your way back to the truth. But what is the truth?

The reason I'm so convinced that if you haven't experienced this yet you will, is because I've had these "I failed" conversations with other biblical counselors, not just Ashley. Thankfully, through the work of the Holy Spirit, whether I'm the one who feels like a failure or I'm the sympathetic co-laborer, the truth always surfaces. And that truth is that God is sovereign, we are not. Just as I often think about a particular detail in the life of Thomas Edison, I also think often about a particular detail concerning the Holy Spirit. It is HE that brings about change in the heart of the counselee, not me, not you. Do you believe that?

We know from Romans 8:11 that it is the role of the Holy Spirit to bring about change.
"If the Spirit of him who raised Jesus from the dead dwells in you, he who raised Christ Jesus from the dead will also give life to your mortal bodies through his Spirit who dwells in you."

But, what does that look like? Let's look at John 3:1-8.

> *Now there was a man of the Pharisees named Nicodemus, a ruler of the Jews. This man came to Jesus by night and said to him, "Rabbi, we know that you are a teacher come from God, for no one can do these signs that you do unless God is with him." Jesus answered him, "Truly, truly, I say to you, unless one is born again he cannot see the kingdom of God." Nicodemus said to him, "How can a man be born when he is old? Can he enter a second time into his mother's womb and be born?" Jesus answered, "Truly, truly, I say to you, unless one is born of water and the Spirit, he cannot enter the kingdom of God. That which is born of the flesh is flesh, and that which is born of the Spirit is spirit. Do*

not marvel that I said to you, 'You must be born again.' The wind
blows where it wishes, and you hear its sound, but you do not
know where it comes from or where it goes. So it is with everyone
who is born of the Spirit."

Let's concentrate on three things Jesus says about the work of the wind, which is a picture of the work of the Spirit. 1) *"The wind blows where it wishes."* In other words, the wind (the Spirit) is free, he is not constrained by us. 2) *"And you hear its sound,"* meaning while the wind (the Spirit) is invisible, there are perceptible effects. We can't see the wind but we can see the effects of the wind as the trees sway and leaves float to the ground. In the same manner, we can't see the Spirit but we can see the effects of him working in the lives of God's children. 3) *"But you do not know where it comes from or where it goes."* This reminds us that we do not originate, control or dictate the destination of the Spirit's movement in our lives or the lives of anyone else.

This is so freeing, isn't it? When a counselee rejects truth, continues on a path of destruction, ignores our counsel or leaves when there is still work to be done, we can release ourselves from feeling like a failure. It is not we who change the counselee. We can, through the power of the Holy Spirit, say all the right words, dig into the most applicable scriptures, pray on bended knees and still not see change. The heart of our counselee is not in our hands. The change that we desperately want to see is not up to us. All we can do is be faithful and leave the work of change in the only capable hands, those of the Holy Spirit.

What if you're not faithful? This leads me to the second aspect of failure. What if you say all the wrong things, lose patience with your counselee, never open your Bible and forego prayer? What about instances like that? Then you have actually failed, right? Even then, my friends, the Spirit can bring counselees to faith, lead them to repentance or give them a moment of clarity in their sanctification. Your being faithful is between you and God. Your counselee changing is between them and the Holy Spirit. Why? The wind blows where it wishes, and you hear its sound, but you do not know where it comes from or where it goes.

What's the point then? Why bring your A game if your efforts aren't what bring change?

Let's consider three reasons.

1. We bring our A game because we live our lives to glorify him, to please him, and to witness to his amazing grace. Consider 2 Corinthians 5:9, " *So whether we are at home or away, we make it our aim to please him.*"

2. We do what we do to the best of our ability because we want to give all our counselees the opportunity to hear the good news of the gospel as stated in Romans 10:14, *"How then will they call on him in whom they have not believed? And how are they to believe in him of whom they have never heard? And how are they to hear without someone preaching?"*

3. We do what we do in order to plant seeds or water seedlings as inspired by 1 Corinthians 3:6, *"I planted, Apollos watered, but God gave the growth."*

Before my arthritis made me scale back on my gardening, I would kneel, place a seed in the ground and pray over it. I thanked God for the way he makes things grow. As the sprouts poked through the dirt, I would pray and thank God for how he provides for us through these tiny, delicate plants. When it rained, I thanked him for watering the seeds and when it was time for the harvest, I thanked him for his abundant love and provision. I'm always amazed that a giant watermelon, a slender carrot, or a spicy pepper can come from a tiny seed that could easily be overlooked, trampled on, or discarded.

I think about this often in the context of counseling. Whether we do our best or our worst in the counseling room, we can trust that if God wants seeds to be planted, they will be planted. If there are seeds that need watering, God will allow our words to saturate the soil and hydrate those seeds. And because God is all powerful and is in no way reliant on us, we can toss seeds in a haphazard manner and allow our watering can to sit empty, but God will cause those seeds to grow if he wills them to do so.

In other words, when Ashley thinks back on her time with Olivia, she *should* consider if she could have done things differently. She *should* ask herself tough questions about how she handled herself in the counseling room. But then she needs to trust God with Olivia's soul. She has to trust that if God allows seeds to be planted, he will bring someone else into her life to water them and in his perfect time, Olivia will bear fruit.

It isn't always easy to trust God, is it? Not because we don't think he can do the work, but because we want things to happen in our timing. We want to plant the seeds, water them and also be there for the harvest. But that just isn't the way it always works. I met a woman about seventeen years ago who thought she knew the Lord, but it was evident that she didn't. I shared the gospel with her multiple times over the years, I prayed for her and with her, I poured into her in a way I've never done before. And guess what? She moved several hours away and about five years ago the Lord opened her eyes, softened her heart, and gave her the gift of saving faith. But I wasn't there for it. All the seeds I had planted over the years were watered by someone else. God caused the growth, not me.

This is the same with Olivia. She and Ashley may see each other in heaven one day and Ashley can rejoice in the Lord knowing that even if she had done things differently, she was intended to be a seed planter. Someone else over the years was sent to water those seeds and God, in his loving kindness, allowed there to be fruit. But what if Ashley doesn't see Olivia in heaven? Were her efforts in vain?

No. Again, ultimately we do what we do to please God and glorify him. But let's also consider the words of Randy Alcorn: *"The best of life on Earth is a glimpse of Heaven; the worst of life is a glimpse of Hell. For Christians, this present life is the closest they will come to Hell. For unbelievers, it is the closest they will come to Heaven."*[20] This quote makes me think that when an unbeliever comes to us for counseling, it is nothing short of God's grace that brought them there. Even if their eyes will never be opened, their hearts never softened and the gift of salvation never given, they were given a glimpse of heaven through you as their biblical counselor. They were pointed to their creator even if they will never come to know him personally, trust in him, or serve him. Their coming to you was no mistake. Your investment in them was not wasted. You can trust that your efforts brought glory to your heavenly Father.

I sincerely hope you have been freed from any guilt you may have been carrying due to a wayward counselee. If indeed you feel you have failed in some way, such as by not putting forth your best efforts, take that to the throne of grace. Trust that your loving, gracious, heavenly Father is faithful to forgive, and trust him with your counselee.

---

[20] Randy Alcorn, *Heaven* (Carol Stream, Illinois: Tyndale House Publishers, Inc., 2004), 28.

A truth we need to keep at the forefronts of our minds is Ephesians 2:8-9, *"For by grace you have been saved through faith. And this is not your own doing; it is the gift of God, not a result of works, so that no one may boast."* God allows us to play a part in the lives of our counselees, but their salvation, their change of heart, and their walking the path of righteousness is not up to us. I can't boast about my friend receiving salvation, but I can rejoice that the Lord allowed me to sow seeds and be a part of her testimony. Again, it is another act of grace by our Heavenly Father.

We also need to understand that when we don't put forth our best efforts, God's will is not hindered. We can't do anything to disrupt his will or cause him to consider a plan B. There is no plan B. Our obedience will keep us in step with the Spirit, just as our lack of obedience will take us out of step with the Spirit. We may rob ourselves of blessings and we may not give our best representation of God's love to our counselees, but we can do nothing to change the outcome of where they will spend eternity. In the same way, we can do nothing, absolutely nothing, to separate ourselves from the love of God, as we are told in Romans 8:35-39.

Praise God!

Let's take another look at the account of the Israelites. Moses and Aaron give us the perfect example of what we've been discussing. Please read along with me, starting in Numbers 20:2-13.

> *Now there was no water for the community, and the people gathered in opposition to Moses and Aaron. They quarreled with Moses and said, "If only we had died when our brothers fell dead before the Lord! Why did you bring the Lord's community into this wilderness, that we and our livestock should die here? Why did you bring us up out of Egypt to this terrible place? It has no*

grain or figs, grapevines or pomegranates. And there is no water to
drink!"

Moses and Aaron went from the assembly to the entrance to the
tent of meeting and fell facedown, and the glory of the Lord
appeared to them. The Lord said to Moses, "Take the staff, and
you and your brother Aaron gather the assembly together. Speak
to that rock before their eyes and it will pour out its water. You
will bring water out of the rock for the community so they and
their livestock can drink."

So Moses took the staff from the Lord's presence, just as he
commanded him. He and Aaron gathered the assembly together in
front of the rock and Moses said to them, "Listen, you rebels,
must we bring you water out of this rock?" Then Moses raised his
arm and struck the rock twice with his staff. Water gushed out,
and the community and their livestock drank.

But the Lord said to Moses and Aaron, "Because you did not
trust in me enough to honor me as holy in the sight of the
Israelites, you will not bring this community into the land I give
them."

These were the waters of Meribah, where the Israelites quarreled
with the Lord and where he was proved holy among them.

By this time in the narrative, Moses and Aaron had been through a lot.
I don't envy the road they'd been traveling. They had seen the Israelites
repeatedly disobey, disrespect and rebel against God. But they had also
seen the people rejoice, worship and honor the Lord, and as a result the
Lord did some amazing things for them. However, just as they were
quick to turn away from doing what was right, so were Moses and
Aaron. We see them here receiving a direct order from God to *speak* to
the rock in order to bring forth water. But, what did Moses do? He

struck the rock. And because God knows the heart of man, he knew this was a trust issue. Moses and Aaron did not trust God; they took matters into their own hands.

I want to point out two important things here. First, God is so kind. The Israelites were not only grumbling once again, Moses and Aaron intentionally disobeyed God also. Yet God still provided them with water. We serve a God that is more gracious than we will ever understand or recognize this side of heaven. Secondly, while God is gracious he is also just. Therefore Moses and Aaron were not only stripped of the privilege of leading the people into the promised land, they themselves didn't even get to go.

Let's look at Numbers 20:22-29.

> *The whole Israelite community set out from Kadesh and came to Mount Hor. At Mount Hor, near the border of Edom, the Lord said to Moses and Aaron, "Aaron will be gathered to his people. He will not enter the land I give the Israelites, because both of you rebelled against my command at the waters of Meribah. Get Aaron and his son Eleazar and take them up Mount Hor. Remove Aaron's garments and put them on his son Eleazar, for Aaron will be gathered to his people; he will die there."*
>
> *Moses did as the Lord commanded: They went up Mount Hor in the sight of the whole community. Moses removed Aaron's garments and put them on his son Eleazar. And Aaron died there on top of the mountain. Then Moses and Eleazar came down from the mountain, and when the whole community learned that Aaron had died, all the Israelites mourned for him thirty days."*

Now let's read Deuteronomy 32:48-52.

Now the Lord spoke to Moses that very same day, saying, "Go up to this mountain of the Abarim, Mount Nebo, which is in the land of Moab opposite Jericho, and look at the land of Canaan, which I am giving to the sons of Israel as a possession. Then you are to die on the mountain where you ascend, and be gathered to your people, as Aaron your brother died on Mount Hor and was gathered to his people, because you broke faith with me in the midst of the sons of Israel at the waters of Meribah-kadesh, in the wilderness of Zin, because you did not treat Me as holy in the midst of the sons of Israel. For you will see the land at a distance but you will not go there, into the land which I am giving the sons of Israel."

This account makes me want to weep. In part because I see how far Moses and Aaron had traveled, how much they had put up with. But not only that. My human, selfish nature thinks it's unfair that they were not allowed to enter the promised land. I tell myself I can feel their disappointment and hear their lament. Yet, I also think my emotions are stirred because I see myself in all these people: in the Israelites, in Moses, and in Aaron. I don't always trust God in the counseling room and I take matters into my own hands as if I know best, as if my way is more effective and as if I can save and bring about change. I recognize my own disobedience in this and my lack of trust in God. Because of this I, like Moses and Aaron, have tasted the loss of blessings that I thought were mine. I've squandered opportunities that the Spirit has put before me, realizing that this also means I've caused others to miss out on blessings as well.

My sin makes me want to weep as does the deep, deep love of our Heavenly Father. Join me in reading Joshua 1:1-5.

After the death of Moses the servant of the Lord, the Lord said to Joshua the son of Nun, Moses' assistant, "Moses my servant is dead. Now therefore arise, go over this Jordan, you and all this people, into the land that I am giving to them, to the people of Israel. Every place that the sole of your foot will tread upon I have given to you, just as I promised to Moses. From the wilderness and this Lebanon as far as the great river, the river Euphrates, all the land of the Hittites to the Great Sea toward the going down of the sun shall be your territory. No man shall be able to stand before you all the days of your life. Just as I was with Moses, so I will be with you. I will not leave you or forsake you."

We do not command the destiny of our counselees. We can be obedient to God and give our all to the task before us, and the eyes of our counselee never be opened. We can follow every prompting from the Holy Spirit and he still may not bring about change in their lives. We can neglect our role as a biblical counselor, be disobedient to God and ignore every prompting from the Holy Spirit and God will still keep his promises. Praise be to God!

I hear Romans 6:1 running through my head, *"What shall we say then? Are we to continue in sin that grace may abound?"* By no means! I can't imagine any biblical counselor intentionally neglecting the importance of his or her role, but yet we all fall short. As my supervisor, David Birch, said to me once, "Even the most seasoned biblical counselor is still a sinner." Friends, even on the days that we leave the counseling room feeling like a failure due to our own mistakes or the disobedience of our counselee, God keeps his promises and the Spirit moves according to his will, not ours.

What's in your Toolbox?

When I look at my failures in the counseling room, I can trace them back to a lack of trust. Even in my pride I'm believing the lie that I can trust my own instincts over the ways of the Almighty God. May we fill our hearts with reminders of God's faithfulness so that our lack of trust will grow faint and our reliance on him will be the source of light in all we do.

1. 2 Peter 3:9

"The Lord is not slow to fulfill his promise as some count slowness, but is patient toward you, not wishing that any should perish, but that all should reach repentance."

We don't always understand why the Spirit doesn't bring about change in every counselee and why God doesn't always bring those who are lost to salvation. Rather than feel like a failure when his perfect timing doesn't line up with our desired timing, we need to lean into this verse, trust his timing and his faithfulness to fulfill his promises.

2. James 1:12

"Blessed is the man who remains steadfast under trial, for when he has stood the test he will receive the crown of life, which God has promised to those who love him."

Sometimes being in the role of biblical counselor means being under trial. We bear the burdens of our brothers and sisters in Christ and we long for the eyes to be opened in those who don't yet know him. But we must not grow weary. Remain steadfast and rejoice in the crown of life that has been promised to you.

3. Joshua 21:45

"Not one word of all the good promises that the Lord had made to the house of Israel had failed; all came to pass."

God's promises and his faithfulness to keep them burst forth from every page of the Holy Bible. We've tasted just a morsel of what he has to offer through the account of Moses and the Israelites. May that morsel give you an appetite to trust him more fully with your own life and the lives of your counselees.

4. Isaiah 26:3

"You keep him in perfect peace whose mind is stayed on you, because he trusts in you."

Moses and Aaron didn't trust God after all they had seen him do. We too, are quick to lose trust in him despite all the promises we've seen him fulfill. The next time you're tempted to trust yourself over him, pray and ask him for his perfect peace and that your mind would stay on him and his faithfulness.

5. Deuteronomy 31:8

"It is the Lord who goes before you. He will be with you; he will not leave you or forsake you. Do not fear or be dismayed."

The next time you enter the counseling room, remind yourself that God is already there. You don't have to fear that you will "do it wrong" or "mess them up even more." God is faithful, he is able, and you can take him at his word.

6. Psalm 37: 23-24

"The steps of a man are established by the Lord, when he delights in his way; though he fall, he shall not be cast headlong, for the Lord upholds his hand."

You aren't always going to say the right thing at the right time. You will fall as every biblical counselor before you has fallen. But take heart, the Lord will uphold you with his mighty hand and he will fulfill his promises despite your mistakes.

7. 2 Corinthians 12:9

"But he said to me, 'My grace is sufficient for you, for my power is made perfect in weakness.' Therefore I will boast all the more gladly of my weaknesses, so that the power of Christ may rest upon me."

I urge you to enter the counseling room fully aware of your weaknesses and equally aware that the power of Christ is resting upon you. You are not sufficient but his grace is.

Encouragement

May you rest easy knowing that God will not call you to do something and then not equip you for the work. Yes, we can use the tools he's equipped us with or we can ignore them, but he is faithful to fulfill his promises. His sovereign will is not dependent on us, however he is gracious and allows us to take part in his plan. I pray this drives us all to our knees and directly to the toolbox that he has given us in his Word.

- **We may fail but He never will**

1 Kings 8:56 says, *"Blessed be the Lord who has given rest to his people Israel, according to all that he promised. Not one word has failed of all his good promise, which he spoke by Moses his servant."*

The next time you feel you've failed your counselee, take that disappointment to God. Remind yourself of all he brought the Israelites through despite their failures. Calm yourself with the truth that he is faithful to you despite your failures. Not one word has failed of all his promises toward the people of Israel nor will one word fail of his promises toward you.

- **He keeps his promises!**

2 Corinthians 1:20 reminds us, *"For all the promises of God find their Yes in him. That is why it is through him that we utter our Amen to God for his glory."*

Friends, we may have counselees who walk out, give up and quit on us, but God never will. I never tire of saying the words "He keeps his promises," and that is why through him we utter our Amen. Because when we utter our Amen we are expressing our confidence that he hears our prayers and will respond according to his sovereign will. He, above all, can be trusted.

- **He is with you always!**

Read Haggai 2:4-5 with me.

"Yet now be strong, O Zerubbabel, declares the Lord. Be strong, O Joshua, son of Jehozadak, the high priest. Be strong, all you people of the land, declares the Lord. Work, for I am with you, declares the Lord of hosts, according to the covenant that I made with you when you came out of Egypt. My Spirit remains in your midst. Fear not."

God made a covenant with us, as his children. His Spirit not only remains in our midst, but he dwells in us! We can go about our work as biblical counselors without fear because he is with us and we can trust him.

Personal Reflections

1. Write about a time when you felt like a failure in the counseling room.

2. What truths in God's Word did you turn to for comfort or perspective?

3. Explain your understanding of how the Spirit is the one who brings about change in the counselee.

4. After going through the account of Moses and the Israelites, who do you find yourself relating to the most? Why do you think this is the case?

5. Make a list or a journal entry of ways you've seen God keep his promises not only in your personal life, but in your journey as a biblical counselor.

6. How does being reminded of God's faithfulness in the past help you trust him more moving forward?

Chapter 10

Counting the Cost

When Christ calls a man, he bids him come and die.
Deitrich Bonhoeffer, *The Cost of Discipleship*

Several years ago I was walking through the hallway of the church that hosted our homeschooling co-op. There was a table along the wall holding resources such as giveaway Bibles, tracks and issues of different Christian magazines. As I glanced at the table, the cover of one of the magazines caught my eye. The woman in the cover photo was so beautiful, so captivating that I stopped mid stride, turned and went back to the table for a better look. I couldn't take my eyes off this woman's smile and her eyes! Her eyes twinkled like nothing I had ever seen. Her beauty was more than the airbrushed images we might expect to see on the cover of Glamour or Vogue. Her beauty was natural and intoxicating in a way I can't even put into words. I just remember thinking, as I inched closer to the table, that I wanted to look as happy and beautiful as this young woman.

It took several seconds of staring at this woman before I noticed her skin was disfigured, her smile wasn't straight and her eyes, while they sparkled, were stretched and a bit gray. One glance at the top of the magazine revealed I was looking at the *Voice of the Martyrs*. This breathtakingly beautiful woman was the victim of a hate crime. She had been burned because of her faith in Jesus Christ. Her village had been attacked, her home destroyed and her body left covered in scars. Yet, the smile on her face displayed unspeakable joy for the suffering she had endured for His name.

After all these years, I can't tell you this woman's name, the location of her village or even the country she was living in, but her image is etched in my memory. I have often thought of the glorious day when I get to meet this sweet sister of mine and tell her how her faith spurred me on, how her joy in the Lord made her scars beautiful and displayed the work of the Holy Spirit in a way that leads my heart to worship. This young woman, like so many around the world, knows all too well the cost of following Jesus.

It's a strange thing to be thankful for living in a country free from this sort of extreme religious persecution and at the same time be envious. Not envious of the persecution per se, but of the spiritual growth that must happen in those instances. I recently read *Forgotten God* by Francis Chan and was moved by a story he recounted about twenty-three missionaries who were held hostage by the Taliban in Afghanistan in 2007. These missionaries were held captive for forty days, two of them being killed by the Taliban before they were released after striking a deal with their homeland of South Korea.[21]

What struck me about this story weren't the horrors they faced while imprisoned or the reality they faced in knowing martyrdom was likely their future. I wasn't even surprised to hear that they had torn a Bible into twenty-three pieces so that they could each glance at the Scriptures while the guards weren't looking. What struck me was what came after

---

[21] Francis Chan (with Danae Yankoski), *Forgotten God: Reversing Our Tragic Neglect of the Holy Spirit* (Colorado Springs, Colorado: David C. Cook, 2009), 107-108.

they were released and allowed to return home. Several of the team members who had been held prisoner asked each other, "Don't you wish we were still there?" They had experienced a deep intimacy with God while being held captive that they had never felt before or since. They so longed to once more feel that intimacy with the Lord that they desired to be back in the brutal conditions of a Taliban prison cell. These people not only knew the cost of following Jesus but were more satisfied while being asked to count that cost.

The persecution we face here in America is vastly different from what our brothers and sisters around the world continue to face. But that doesn't mean we aren't asked to count the cost of following Jesus. I know people whose family ties have been cut, marriages broken and relationships severed once a confession of faith in the Lord was made. I'm reminded of Jackie, a counselee who once told me, with tears in her eyes, that her life was easier before she became a Christian. Her circle of friends had changed due to her change in values, but she missed those friends and often felt lonely. Her parents refused to discuss her faith and wouldn't attend her baptism. While she rejoiced in her gift of saving faith, she was devastated by the realization that her family had not yet received that gift. Her mind was flooded with thoughts of not spending eternity with her family. She was overwhelmed with questions about how God could possibly wipe away those tears in the hereafter. Jackie was in the process of counting the cost of following Jesus. Can you relate to Jackie? Have you ever felt your life was easier before knowing the Lord? Let's consider Jesus' words in Luke 14:25-33.

> Now great crowds accompanied him, and he turned and said to them, "If anyone comes to me and does not hate his own father and mother and wife and children and brothers and sisters, yes, and even his own life, he cannot be my disciple. Whoever does not bear his own cross and come after me cannot be my disciple. For

which of you, desiring to build a tower, does not first sit down and
count the cost, whether he has enough to complete it? Otherwise,
when he has laid a foundation and is not able to finish, all who see
it begin to mock him, saying, 'This man began to build and was
not able to finish.' Or what king, going out to encounter another
king in war, will not sit down first and deliberate whether he is
able with ten thousand to meet him who comes against him with
twenty thousand? And if not, while the other is yet a great way
off, he sends a delegation and asks for terms of peace. So therefore,
any one of you who does not renounce all that he has cannot be my
disciple."

This passage brings the film *Amazing Grace* to mind. This film, set in the 18th century, depicts the life and conversion of politician William Wilberforce. One scene shows William sitting on the lawn studying dandelions and marveling at God's creativity in the spinning of spider webs. William's butler, Richard, approaches him on the lawn, since William has places to be and people to see. But as it happens, God has other plans. William tries explaining to his butler, "It's God," and though he has 10,000 engagements of state that day, he would rather spend the day sitting on the lawn taking in God's handiwork. The butler asks, "You found God, sir?" William responds by saying, "I think he found me. You have any idea how inconvenient that is?"

If you've ever studied the life of William Wilberforce, you know that he led a life of sacrifice in response to his faith. Before his conversion he admittedly lived his life the way he pleased, spending his time and money for his own benefit and enjoyment. In fact, journals show William describing his young adult years as a waste of precious time, opportunity and talents. But, after God took hold of his heart, there was radical change. The Spirit impressed upon William to love God and to love his neighbor as himself, and thus he spent twenty years of his life fighting to abolish the British slave trade. When the victory finally came, he spent an additional twenty-six years implementing the abolition of the slave trade and fighting to abolish slavery altogether in the British colonies. After forty six years, slavery was finally outlawed just three days before the Lord took William home. How gracious was our God to allow William to see the fruits of his labor!

William counted the cost, and he devoted his life to what he felt the Lord had called him to do. If someone were to find your journals generations from now, would they say the same about you?
I ask this because just as my counselee, Jackie, said that her life was easier before she became a Christian, I can say my life was easier before I started serving as a biblical counselor. Bearing the heavy burdens of others is no small task. Yet, despite the heartache, discouragement, anxiety and tears, serving in this capacity has been more fulfilling than I could have ever imagined. Not because I walk away feeling good about myself at the end of each session; quite the contrary. I find fulfillment in watching God work. I find my faith increasing as he works through me despite my inadequacies.

I'm confident that when William started fighting to abolish slavery, he was under no delusion that it would be a short and easy fight. He may not have known from day one that he would be giving forty-six years of his life to this one task, but he was faithful to the task nonetheless. He kept giving of himself. He kept loving God and others. Friends, what we have to remember is that when we choose to follow Jesus we must count the cost. Likewise, we must count the cost of serving as biblical counselors.

By the work of the Holy Spirit, William Wilberforce's faith was spurred into action by the command to love your God with all your heart and to love your neighbor as yourself (Mark 12:30-31). Think back to what first piqued your interest in becoming a biblical counselor. What was it? Was it this very command? Was it a particular sermon? A notion that God placed on your heart? Perhaps you were once on the receiving end of biblical counseling and seeing God's powerful hand in your own life led you to join him in this kingdom work.

Take time to reflect on what led you down this road. Has the road been smooth or scattered with bumps and potholes? Now that you're actively counseling, have you found yourself wondering what in the world you've agreed to? Have you been surprised at how difficult the work can be? My encouragement to you is the same encouragement I gave Jackie. The young woman whose body was burned because of her faith is able to smile and exude joy because of the Holy Spirit in her. The Holy Spirit is what allowed those missionaries to long for the Taliban prison in order to, once again, experience deep intimacy with the Lord. William Wilberforce devoted his life to freeing people he had never met because of a conviction from the indwelling Holy Spirit. Friends, it is the same Holy Spirit that resides in us and because of his immeasurable love and grace, we are able to serve. We are able to bear the burdens of others and endure everything that comes our way. It is by drawing on his strength that we can endure and serve joyfully.

As we've followed the account of Moses and the Israelites, we've had many opportunities to relate their story to our own. With each passing chapter I've seen more and more clearly that when we follow Jesus into the counseling room we're accepting the fact that he's asking us to walk in the desert. While in the desert we will likely walk with counselees who rejoice and sing praises and even dance with their tambourines. But there will also be times when we walk with those who lie, manipulate, gossip, slander, hate and bow down to worship golden calves. There will be times of thirst and hunger and we will learn new ways to wait and rely on God, our provider. There will be times when we are tongue-tied and he will provide someone else to speak for us. We will experience loss and we will also see new life. We will encounter God in new ways and we will long to be closer still. We will worship, we will pray and we will, at times, be unfaithful. But he will go before us, guiding and leading us through the work he has laid out. And as our time in the desert draws to an end, if he so desires, he will raise up someone else to pick up where we left off. He is our God and he is ever faithful.

While our walk in the desert is vastly different from that of Moses, I pray you can see the similarities and what we can learn from his account. Let's consider Paul's words in 1 Corinthians 10:1-13.

> For I do not want you to be unaware, brothers, that our fathers were all under the cloud, and all passed through the sea, and all were baptized into Moses in the cloud and in the sea, and all ate the same spiritual food, and all drank the same spiritual drink. For they drank from the spiritual Rock that followed them, and the Rock was Christ. Nevertheless, with most of them God was not pleased, for they were overthrown in the wilderness.

> Now these things took place as examples for us, that we might not desire evil as they did. Do not be idolaters as some of them were; as it is written, "The people sat down to eat and drink and rose up to play." We must not indulge in sexual immorality as some of them did, and twenty-three thousand fell in a single day. We must not put Christ to the test, as some of them did and were destroyed by serpents, nor grumble, as some of them did and were destroyed by the Destroyer. Now these things happened to them as an example, but they were written down for our instruction, on whom the end of the ages has come. Therefore let anyone who thinks that he stands take heed lest he fall. No temptation has overtaken you

that is not common to man. God is faithful, and he will not let
you be tempted beyond your ability, but with the temptation he will
also provide the way of escape, that you may be able to endure it.

Friends, the longer we serve as biblical counselors the more creative the enemy will become. Between our enemy and our own sinful flesh, the temptations will not only keep coming, but will likely magnify. Praise God we can revisit accounts like those of Moses and learn from the examples we see there. When we find ourselves regretting the past and are tempted to dwell on our mistakes, we can look to the one who redeems our past and holds our future. When we see change in ourselves and are tempted to grumble over the lack of change in those around us, we can look to the author and perfecter of our faith. We can trust him with our own souls and the souls of those we love. When dread sets in and we're tempted to quit, we can draw strength from the One who gives us living water.

When expectations aren't met and we start to doubt, we can rest in God's perfect plan. When we, as counselors, need counseling and we doubt our ability to serve, we can look to the Comforter and trust that he will care for us. When life gets in the way and we neglect our personal soul care, we can trust that he never neglects us. When we are hit with spiritual warfare and want to throw in the towel, he is faithful to draw us to himself. When the temptation to gossip is all consuming, we can ask him to stand guard over our mouths. When we feel like a failure and are tempted to walk away, we can trust that it is God's plan in play, not our own. And when we count the cost of following him into the counseling room, by the work of the Holy Spirit, we can count that cost with joy rather than resentment.

Should the day come that we must retire from this great work, I pray we will miss the struggle, the heartache and the tears. Because it is there that we found ourselves most intimate with, reliant on and trusting in our Lord and Savior. We can marvel over the young women like the one on the cover of *Voice of the Martyrs* magazine. We can stand in awe of missionaries like the ones who were imprisoned by the Taliban. We can envy the zeal and deep conviction of William Wilberforce and we can study all the many examples given to us by Moses. Yet, at the end of the day, they aren't the example we should be following. Jesus is. He is our guide through the desert.

Look with me at Philippians 2:1-13.

> *So if there is any encouragement in Christ, any comfort from love, any participation in the Spirit, any affection and sympathy, complete my joy by being of the same mind, having the same love, being in full accord and of one mind. Do nothing from selfish ambition or conceit, but in humility count others more significant than yourselves. Let each of you look not only to his own interests, but also to the interests of others. Have this mind among yourselves, which is yours in Christ Jesus, who, though he was in the form of God, did not count equality with God a thing to be grasped, but emptied himself, by taking the form of a servant, being born in the likeness of men. And being found in human form, he humbled himself by becoming obedient to the point of death, even death on a cross. Therefore God has highly exalted him and bestowed on him the name that is above every name, so that at the name of Jesus every knee should bow, in heaven and on earth and under the earth, and every tongue confess that Jesus Christ is Lord, to the glory of God the Father. Therefore, my beloved, as you have always obeyed, so now, not only as in my presence but much more in my absence, work out your own*

salvation with fear and trembling, for it is God who works in you, both to will and to work for his good pleasure.

I remember a year or so ago talking with some other biblical counselors about this very thing: the labor of love we call biblical counseling. We were discussing our love for this great work but also our exhaustion. We shared thoughts on when and how to take a break to rejuvenate and reorient ourselves. But, what we all came back to was this idea presented in Philippians 2. Jesus is our ultimate example. And what example did he give us? He emptied himself, by taking the form of a servant.

We aren't Jesus. Not now, not ever. Yet, while we know this, we can very easily develop a savior complex and think that all the change that happens in our counselees is our doing and if we take a break, the work won't get done. This is another reason our conversations went to Philippians 2, because this section ends with the reminder that it is God who does the work. Jesus is our example to humble and empty ourselves, to live as servants. It is God who equips us for the work, gives us the strength to endure, and works in us, both to will and to work for his good pleasure.

Let's look at Deuteronomy 34:1-4.

> *Then Moses climbed Mount Nebo from the plains of Moab to the top of Pisgah, across from Jericho. There the Lord showed him the whole land—from Gilead to Dan, all of Naphtali, the territory of Ephraim and Manasseh, all the land of Judah as far as the Mediterranean Sea, the Negev and the whole region from the Valley of Jericho, the City of Palms, as far as Zoar. Then the Lord said to him, "This is the land I promised on oath to*

Abraham, Isaac and Jacob when I said, 'I will give it to your descendants.'"

We know that Moses wasn't allowed to enter the promised land, but I love this image of Moses climbing to the top of a mountain. I picture him sitting down to catch his breath and then losing his breath all over again as he looks out on the land the Lord had promised his descendants. What a view that must have been! What an astounding sight for Moses to behold!

Friends, I want to encourage you with the astounding sight that we will one day behold. Because God is a gift giver, I can't help but think he will allow us to know whose salvation story we were a part of: family, friends, strangers perhaps, but most certainly our counselees. We will see the fruit from seeds we planted and seeds we watered. We will see the work of the Holy Spirit in all its splendor. And when we are rewarded for our labor, through the work of Jesus Christ, we will take those rewards and lay them at Jesus' feet. What a glorious day that will be. What a glorious life we will have lived serving in this capacity.

What's in your Toolbox?

As we count the cost of not only following Jesus, but serving him as biblical counselors, we need to prepare for trials. The good news is, just as our trials are no surprise to God, they shouldn't be a surprise to us. We can expect trials. Inside and outside the counseling room. And by God's grace, he has not only equipped us to face the trials, he uses those trials to grow, strengthen and mature us. Praise be to God!

1. James 1:2-4

"Count it all joy, my brothers, when you meet trials of various kinds, for you know that the testing of your faith produces steadfastness. And let steadfastness have its full effect, that you may be perfect and complete, lacking in nothing."

I was told early on that the more trials I face as a biblical counselor, the more I will get used to it. While that might be true, we must remember, the end goal of facing trials is not endurance, but maturity.

2. Romans 8:28

"And we know that for those who love God all things work together for good, for those who are called according to his purpose."

As we walk with our counselees through their trials and as we face our own, we can know that God is sovereign. Even if we are unsure that our counselee has a saving faith, we can be assured of our own salvation. Because of that we can trust that what we face will be for our good and his glory.

3. James 1:12

"Blessed is the man who remains steadfast under trial, for when he has stood the test he will receive the crown of life, which God has promised to those who love him."

For many years I struggled with being motivated by the promise of receiving the crown of life. Being motivated by rewards seemed wrong. I wanted my motivations to be spurred on by, and only by, my love of the Lord. But as God has grown me up in my faith, I realize now I should be motivated by rewards. Because the more rewards I receive, the more rewards I have to lay at Jesus' feet. May we all remain steadfast under trial and receive the crown of life!

4. Psalm 16:8

"I have set the Lord always before me. Because he is at my right hand, I will not be shaken."

We can trust God to go before us and pave the way. He will sometimes pave the way and smooth the surface as he goes. But other times he will let the path be bumpy. Even still, he is at our right hand and we will not be shaken.

5. Philippians 4:11-13

"Not that I speak from want, for I have learned to be content in whatever circumstances I am. I know how to get along with humble means, and I also know how to live in prosperity; in any and every circumstance I have learned the secret of being filled and going hungry, both of having abundance and suffering need. I can do all things through Him who strengthens me."

While we will likely never experience the dire circumstances Paul did, we have our own seasons of want and need. Praise be to God that, through him, we can do all things. We can endure, remain steadfast in our faith and be content in whatever comes our way.

6. Deuteronomy 31:6-8

"Be strong and bold; have no fear or dread of them, because it is the Lord your God who goes before you. He will be with you; he will not fail you or forsake you. Do not fear or be dismayed."

It's difficult to never have fear or to never be dismayed. We live in a broken world with broken people and we're surrounded by heartache. But, the Lord allows us to see the glory of his creation and the work of his hand. It is the daily reminders of his presence in our lives that allows us to go forth with strength and boldness.

7. Hebrews 12:1

"Therefore, since we are surrounded by such a great cloud of witnesses, let us throw off everything that hinders and the sin that so easily entangles. And let us run with perseverance the race marked out for us."

I was reminded of Enoch and expressed my desire to have his faith. He walked so closely with the Lord, that God just took him (Gen. 5:21-24). Whatever that faith looks like, I want that kind of faith. It was my husband who responded by saying, "You have that kind of faith by persevering. You continue to walk through the hard times knowing he is with you. You make the hard decisions while asking for wisdom. You rely on him to get through your anxiety. You walk in faith. You trust him."

May we all remember those words as we run the race marked out for us.

Encouragement

I've been told I'm not a sugar-coater. And I would agree with that statement. I could have written a book focusing solely on the bountiful riches that come from serving as a biblical counselor. But I feel I have served you better by giving you a raw, non-sugar-coated, look at what you will likely face in the months and years ahead. We shouldn't be afraid to talk about the difficulties of serving as biblical counselors. And we certainly shouldn't shy away from this kingdom work because it can be burdensome. Quite the contrary. Through the grace of our Lord Jesus Christ, we can lean into this work knowing he will carry the burden for us. He will equip us, strengthen us and use all our trials for our sanctification. Knowing what we face is for our good and his glory makes the work seem less like work and more like a willful joining in Christ's suffering.

- **We will suffer!**

Romans 8:16-17, *"The Spirit himself bears witness with our spirit that we are children of God, and if children, then heirs—heirs of God and fellow heirs with Christ, provided we suffer with him in order that we may also be glorified with him."*

Only children of God can put an exclamation point after the words "we will suffer" as if it's something to be celebrated. But according to Romans 8, it is:

As you serve our King, may you see your suffering with him as a precursor to being glorified with him. This truth will give you joy in your suffering.

- **We do not labor in vain!**

1 Corinthians 15:58, *"Therefore, my beloved brothers, be steadfast, immovable, always abounding in the work of the Lord, knowing that in the Lord your labor is not in vain."*

This verse gives me so much hope and I pray it does you too. Whatever we face in the counseling room, as long as we are faithful to point our counselees to the truth of scripture, we can know our labor is not in vain.

- **He has overcome the world!**

John 16:33, *"I have told you these things, so that in me you may have peace. In this world you will have trouble. But take heart! I have overcome the world."*

What beautiful words to end on. We will have trouble in this world. There is no denying that. Trouble will come in our everyday lives and in the counseling room. But, take heart! He has overcome the world!

Personal Reflections

1. Have you had the thought that your life was easier before you started serving as a biblical counselor? What aspects of your life were easier?

2. What are specific ways you draw strength from the Lord to persevere?

3. Write down what originally prompted you to pursue serving as a biblical counselor. Have your motivations changed over time? What are they now?

4. If you were encouraging someone to serve as a biblical counselor, what would you share with them in order to give them an accurate picture of what this kingdom work looks like?

5. Through the trials you've faced in the counseling room, what are some ways you've already seen the Lord redeeming that time? How has he reminded you that you do not labor in vain?

6. Despite the trials you've faced in this service to the Lord, describe some of the amazing ways you've seen the Lord work in your own life and in the lives of your counselees.

Conclusion

There's no way around it, this work is hard. This work is exhausting. There will be days when you want to be doing anything other than serving as a biblical counselor. Yet, I pray the Lord will continue to fill all our hearts with a longing to help others. I ask that he would give us all a desire to empty ourselves as servants. I pray for a longing to sacrifice our own comfort in order to see God at work in the lives of those he brings to us. As you close this book and return to your service to the King, I leave you with these words from Ephesians 3:20-21.

"Now to him who is able to do far more abundantly than all that we ask or think, according to the power at work within us, to him be glory in the church and in Christ Jesus throughout all generations, forever and ever. Amen."

Made in the USA
Monee, IL
19 August 2023

41254150R00108